D1065368

The Bill of Rights

Other titles in *The Constitution:*

The First Amendment
Freedom of Speech, Religion, and the Press
ISBN: 0-89490-897-9

The Second Amendment
The Right to Own Guns
ISBN:0-89490-925-8

The Fourth Amendment
Search and Seizure
ISBN: 0-89490-924-X

The Fifth Amendment
The Right to Remain Silent
ISBN: 0-89490-894-4

The Thirteenth Amendment
Ending Slavery
ISBN: 0-89490-923-1

The Fifteenth Amendment
African-American Men's Right to Vote
ISBN: 0-7660-1033-3

The Eighteenth and Twenty-First Amendments
Alcohol—Prohibition and Repeal
ISBN: 0-89490-926-6

The Nineteenth Amendment
Women's Right to Vote
ISBN: 0-89490-922-3

The Bill of Rights

The First Ten Amendments of the Constitution

David L. Hudson, Jr.

Enslow Publishers, Inc.

40 Industrial Road	PO Box 38
Box 398	Aldershot
Berkeley Heights, NJ 07922	Hants GU12 6BP
USA	UK

http://www.enslow.com

To my parents and John Seigenthaler

Library of Congress Cataloging-in-Publication Data

Hudson, David (David L.), 1969–
    The Bill of Rights : the first ten amendments of the constitution / David Hudson.
        p. cm. — (The Constitution)
        Includes bibliographical references and index.
        Summary: Traces the history of the writing of the first ten amendments to the Constitution, and examines each amendment's provisions and applications in detail.
        ISBN 0-7660-1903-9
        1. United States. Constitution. 1st–10th Amendments—Juvenile literature. 2. Constitutional amendments—United States—Juvenile literature. 3. Civil rights—United States—Juvenile literature. [1. United States. Constitution. 1st–10th Amendments. 2. Constitutional amendments. 3. Civil rights.]
        I. Title. II. Constitution (Springfield, Union County, N.J.)
        KF4750 .H847 2002
        342.73'085—dc21

                                                    2001002900

Printed in the United States of America

10 9 8 7 6 5 4 3 2 1

To Our Readers: We have done our best to make sure all Internet addresses in this book were active and appropriate when we went to press. However, the author and the publisher have no control over and assume no liability for the material available on those Internet sites or on other Web sites they may link to. Any comments or suggestions can be sent by e-mail to comments@enslow.com or to the address on the back cover.

Illustration Credits: Collection of the Supreme Court of the United States, p. 88; © Corel Corporation, p. 19; Harris and Ewing, Collection of the Supreme Court of the United States, p. 71; Independence National Historic Park, p. 56; John Grafton, *The American Revolution: A Picture Sourcebook* (New York: Dover Publications, Inc., 1975), pp. 38, 40; Library of Congress, pp. 11, 16, 45, 54, 92; National Archives, pp. 17; Reproduced from the *Dictionary of American Portraits*, Published by Dover Publications, Inc., in 1967, pp. 42, 44, 48, 51, 62, 63, 67.

Cover Illustration: National Archives

Contents

Introduction

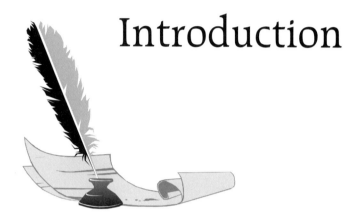

Too often we in the United States take our precious individual liberties for granted. All students and citizens should stop and think for a moment about how the world would be without these liberties.

Consider the following example. A public junior high school teacher assigns her students a creative writing project. The teacher instructs the students that the poem must contain a theme arising out of a major current event that has had a major impact on them. One student decides to write a poem about school violence in the wake of several recent school shootings, including the 1999 tragic school shooting at Columbine High School in Littleton, Colorado.

The poem expresses the inner demons of a student who feels alienated by his peers. In his mind, the student's fictional character debates whether he should become the bully and lash out violently against his tormentors. The teacher mistakenly believes the poem to be a threat. The teacher shows the poem to the principal and school resource officer. The three decide that the student poses an immediate risk to himself and others.

The school officials strip search the student, interrogate him for several hours, and then call the police. The school officials then expel the student permanently, citing a "zero tolerance" policy against violence.

The police interrogate the student for several hours without reading him his rights or allowing him to call his family. They lock the student in a juvenile detention center cell, where he remains incarcerated until an emergency court hearing.

In the meantime, the police enter the student's home, search his room, and seize his home computer without a warrant.

In this scenario, the public school officials and the police violated the student's constitutional rights. They infringed on his freedom of speech, freedom from unreasonable searches and seizures, and freedom from self-incrimination.

What if the police could enter your home at any time for no reason and search through your personal possessions? What if you could be imprisoned merely for writing an article that criticizes a local politician?

Imagine if you could be put to death for a minor criminal offense, such as shoplifting a candy bar. Imagine if you could be thrown in jail, denied an attorney, and not be able to confront your accusers.

Imagine if the government could command that you practice a certain religion or could banish you out of the country. Consider if you could be declared guilty without a jury trial.

Such was—and is—the plight of millions of people in countries all over the globe. Fortunately, in America we have these individual liberties ensured by law. Sometimes, government officials violate people's constitutional rights. But, at least in this country, we usually have a remedy in our United States Constitution.

Our Constitution—and particularly the first ten amendments to the Constitution—provide us with what our fourth President James Madison called "the great rights of mankind." These ten amendments are called the Bill of Rights.

In his book *The Life of the Law,* attorney Al Knight argues that our legal system is the most important and unique part of our culture. He writes: "Nothing like it has ever been seen before on this planet so far as we know. It is distinguished above all else by its breathtaking generosity to the individual."[1]

The Bill of Rights symbolizes this "breathtaking generosity." It safeguards our constitutional rights. United States Supreme Court Justice Hugo Black wrote that the Bill of Rights "protect and safeguard the most cherished liberties of a free people."[2]

What Is the Bill of Rights?

The United States Constitution sets out the structure of our government. It divides various powers among the three branches of the federal government—the executive, legislative and judicial.

The Bill of Rights was added to the Constitution in part to ensure that the powers of the federal government would not trample upon individual liberty.

The first eight amendments to the United States Constitution are designed to protect individuals from abuse by federal government officials. The ninth and tenth amendments set out the division of powers between the federal government and the various state governments. The Fourteenth Amendment ensures that most of the rights contained in the first eight amendments of the Bill of Rights apply to state and local government officials.

The First Amendment

Congress shall make no law respecting an establishment of religion or prohibiting the free exercise thereof; or abridging the freedom of speech, or of the press; or the

right of the people peaceably to assemble, and to
petition the Government for a redress of grievances.

The First Amendment serves as our blueprint for personal freedom. It ensures that we live in an open society. The First Amendment contains five freedoms: religion, speech, press, assembly and petition.

Without the First Amendment, religious minorities could be persecuted or the government could establish a single, national religion. The press could not criticize government and citizens could not mobilize for social change. This would mean we would lose our individual freedom.

Freedom of Religion

The first two clauses of the First Amendment—"respecting an establishment of religion or prohibiting the free exercise thereof"—are the religion clauses. The first is the establishment clause. The second is the free-exercise clause. Together, these clauses require that the government act in a neutral manner when it comes to religion.

The Establishment Clause provides that church and state remain separate to a certain degree. In a letter to the Danbury Baptists in 1802, Thomas Jefferson used the phrase a "wall of separation between church and state." The U.S. Supreme Court used Jefferson's "wall of separation" metaphor to describe the meaning of the establishment clause.[1]

James Madison, Thomas Jefferson, and some of our other Founding Fathers wanted to place some distance between church and state to prevent American political leaders from acting like English monarchs who were intolerant of other religious views.

King Henry VIII was a prime example. He broke away from the Catholic Church in 1531 after the pope refused to support his divorce from Catherine of Aragon. Henry

Henry VIII broke away from the Catholic Church and put himself at the head of the new Church of England, which became the official church of the entire nation.

established the Protestant Church of England. In 1534, the English Parliament passed the Act of Supremacy establishing Henry as the head of the Church of England.

Later, Parliament passed the Treason Act, which effectively silenced anyone who spoke out against the king. The act was used to silence religious dissenters. Religious intolerance seemed to be the standard in much of Europe, including England. Many people fled England to settle in America and the New World because of religious persecution. Religious dissenters in England were ostracized, punished, and imprisoned.

In the 1960s, the United States Supreme Court ruled that public school officials violated the establishment clause when they led students in prayer. The Court explained that a reasonable observer would believe that the school officials were advancing or endorsing a certain religion over other religions. Members of religious minorities would be coerced to conform to the majority religion.

Historians, judges, and members of the public dispute the meaning of the establishment clause. Some believe the clause only meant to prohibit the government from setting up a national church. Others apply the "wall of separation" theory more vigorously and disagree with any state involvement with religion. They argue that the state cannot grant aid to religious institutions. So-called strict separationists oppose school voucher programs in which parents are given tuition monies for their kids to attend certain schools, including parochial (or religious) schools.

The second religion clause of the First Amendment is the free-exercise clause. It protects a person's right to practice religion freely. In 1963, the United States Supreme Court ruled that South Carolina officials violated the free-exercise rights of Adele Sherbert, a Seventh-Day Adventist who was fired from her job and denied unemployment benefits because she would not work on Saturday.[2] Seventh-Day Adventists believe that the day of worship is Saturday, not Sunday.

In 1990, the United States Supreme Court decided a case involving a similar issue. Two Native American drug counselors claimed their First Amendment rights were violated when they were denied unemployment benefits after they were fired for drug use. The individuals had ingested peyote—a hallucinogenic drug—for religious reasons. The two individuals argued that their religious rights, like that of Ms. Sherbert, were being punished.[3]

The Court ruled in favor of the state and against the two former drug counselors. The High Court wrote that the state's criminal law against drug use was a neutral law of general applicability. The Court found there was no religious exemption to fail to comply with the state's drug laws.

Freedom of Speech

The First Amendment protects the right of free speech, even offensive speech. Our early leaders, known as the Founding Fathers, spoke out mightily against arbitrary actions by the king of England and the English Parliament, such as tax increases. They wanted to ensure that Americans would have the right to criticize their government.

Shortly after World War I, many socialists and anarchists, who disagreed with the United States' system of government, were punished for their anti-war speeches and writings. Justice Oliver Wendell Holmes developed the so-called "clear and present danger" test in the case of *Schenck* v. *U.S.* in 1919. Under this standard, a person could not be punished for his or her speech, unless that speech causes a "clear and present danger." For example, the government could prohibit speech that caused an immediate riot.

Freedom of speech also applies to more than just oral

speech. Certain forms of symbolic speech, or expressive conduct, also receive protection. In the 1960s, public high school students in Iowa wore black armbands to school to protest United States' involvement in the Vietnam War. The Supreme Court determined in 1969 that the students' act of wearing the armbands was "closely akin" to pure speech.[4]

Similarly, in 1984, Gregory "Joey" Johnson burned an American flag outside the Republican National Convention as a form of political protest. In a 1989 decision, the Supreme Court determined that the act of burning the flag was a form of free expression. The Court held that burning the flag, like wearing the black armbands, was an effective means of communicating a certain message.

Not all speech, however, receives protection. Certain forms of speech receive no protection. These categories include obscenity and "fighting words." Obscenity refers to speech that depicts sexual activities in a graphic way. Fighting words refers to face-to-face insults that cause an immediate violent reaction. The United States Supreme Court has determined that these types of speech are harmful and do not contribute meaningfully to the marketplace of ideas.

Some people claim that hate speech—speech that targets a particular group because of race or religion— should also be prohibited. Even hateful speech receives protection under the First Amendment unless it incites imminent, or immediate, lawless action.

Freedom of the Press

Thomas Jefferson once said that if he had to choose between a government without newspapers, or newspapers without government, he would not hesitate to "choose the latter."[5]

A free press is the heart of the First Amendment. The press has historically served as a check upon the government. The press is sometimes referred to as the Fourth

Estate because of its important position in society in examining the three branches of government—the executive, legislative, and judicial. The press in England was not free. English officials passed licensing laws that forced writers and publishers to obtain prior approval of their works from the crown before publication.

The English monarchy established this system of prior restraint in order to prevent criticism of the king. English courts, including the secret court known as the Star Chamber, punished those who engaged in seditious libel. In theory, seditious libel referred to speech that called for treason against the government. In practice, seditious libel referred to speech criticizing the king.

In this country, the tradition of press freedom began with the celebrated case in 1734 of John Peter Zenger, who was prosecuted for criminal libel for criticizing the royal governor of New York, William Cosby. In a landmark legal moment, a jury ignored the prevailing law at the time and determined that truth was a defense to a libel action. Under current law, truth is a defense to libel.

More than two hundred years later, in 1964, the United States Supreme Court afforded the press much greater freedom in *New York Times Co. v. Sullivan.*[6] In this case, *The New York Times* printed an editorial advertisement by the "Committee to Defend Martin Luther King and the Struggle for Freedom in the South."

The ad criticized the actions of certain "Southern violators" and accused them of violating the civil rights of African-American students in Montgomery, Alabama. The ad read: "Again and again the Southern violators have answered Dr. King's peaceful protests with intimidation and violence. They have bombed his home almost killing his wife and child. They have assaulted his person. They have arrested him seven times."[7]

Even though he was not named specifically in the ad, L. B. Sullivan, the Montgomery, Alabama, city commissioner in charge of the police, sued the newspaper for libel (publishing false statements of facts about someone). The article contained certain misstatements. For example, Dr. King had been arrested only four times, not seven.

An Alabama jury awarded Sullivan $500,000. However, the United States Supreme Court reversed the jury verdict against the newspaper. The decision "transformed American libel law."[8] The Court wrote that "debate on public issues should be uninhibited, robust, and wide-open, and . . . may well include vehement, caustic, and sometimes unpleasantly sharp attacks on government and public officials."[9]

Now, the press faces lawsuits for allegedly violating people's right to privacy. Celebrities and private individuals sometimes contend that the press goes too far in

Martin Luther King, Jr., used peaceful protest to try to win civil rights for African Americans.

disclosing private information. Ellen Alderman and Caroline Kennedy describe this phenomenon as "a clash between the right to be let alone and the right to know, a clash between privacy and the press."[10]

Freedom of Assembly and Petition

The last two freedoms of the First Amendment ensure that citizens can assemble together and directly petition the government to call public attention to a certain cause.

Over the course of American history, striking workers, civil rights advocates, antiwar demonstrators, and Ku Klux Klan marchers have sought the protections of the First Amendment. They sought the right to freely assemble and petition the government for a redress of grievances. Sometimes these efforts have galvanized public support or changed public perceptions. The freedom of assembly was essential to both the civil rights movement of the 1950s and 1960s and the women's suffrage movement.

Citizens also have a right to petition the government to correct injustices, or in the words of the First Amendment, for a "redress of grievances." Though probably the least

Despite the fact that many people disagree strongly with their views on race and ethnicity, members of the Ku Klux Klan have the right under the First Amendment to march peacefully to express their opinions.

known clause of the First Amendment, it arguably has deeper historical roots than any other First Amendment freedom. Consider that two of history's most venerated documents—the Magna Carta and the Declaration of Independence—were petitions to kings of England. Each document petitioned the ruler with various complaints.

The Second Amendment

> A well regulated Militia, being necessary to the security of a free State, the right of the people to keep and bear Arms, shall not be infringed.

Most of the provisions of the Bill of Rights can be traced to freedoms first developed in England. The English Bill of Rights of 1689 declares that individuals should have the right to bear arms.

The great English legal historian William Blackstone wrote in his *Commentaries on the Laws of England* that the right to bear arms was necessary "to protect and maintain inviolate the three great and primary rights of personal security, personal liberty, and private property."[11]

Americans in the late eighteenth century viewed the right to bear arms as necessary for liberty. Colonists needed firearms for hunting. They also needed weapons when they confronted hostile strangers or foreign enemies in the New World. The right to bear arms was explicitly mentioned in the early state constitutions of Pennsylvania, North Carolina, Vermont, and Massachusetts.[12]

Legal historians debate whether the amendment applies to a collective or individual right. In other words, historians differ on whether the right to bear arms applies to a militia or to each individual. The dispute occurs because the wording of the amendment begins with a preamble mentioning "a well regulated militia."[13]

Today, many Americans still own guns for recreation and personal safety. They view the federal government

There is strong disagreement among Americans over whether the Second Amendment protects the right of all individuals to own guns, or whether the provision refers to militias alone.

and its laws regulating the sale of handguns and other firearms as infringing on personal freedom. The National Rifle Association (NRA), for instance, is a powerful group that lobbies against many gun-control laws and on behalf of citizen's Second Amendment rights.

The downside for many government officials is the high number of handgun deaths each year in the United States—more than any other country not at war in the world. Recent school shootings have increased public awareness about firearms. Many believe that we must limit firearms in the stream of commerce.

The Third Amendment

No Soldier shall, in time of peace be quartered in any house, without the consent of the Owner, nor in time of war, but in a manner to be prescribed by law.

The Founding Fathers adopted this amendment to prevent the federal government from housing troops in individuals' homes. In colonial times, the British government would house (or quarter) troops in colonists' homes without their consent. The Quartering Act of 1765 allowed the English to house troops in colonists' homes.

This is the least significant provision of the Bill of Rights for the modern world. Today members of the armed forces live in communities and on military bases, not in the private homes of nonmilitary citizens.

The Fourth Amendment

> The right of the people to be secure in their persons, houses, papers and effects, against unreasonable searches and seizures, shall not be violated, and no Warrants shall issue, but upon probable cause, supported by Oath or affirmation, and particularly describing the place to be searched, and the persons or things to be seized.

A popular saying is a "man's home is his castle." The Constitution safeguards this concept of privacy in the Fourth Amendment. This amendment protects people from government invasions into their homes and bodies.

During the colonial period, British custom officials would obtain search warrants called writs of assistance. These writs allowed the officials to inspect all of a colonist's cargo to prevent smuggling of goods that were to be taxed. These writs of assistance allowed the officials to search and seize whatever property they desired without prior approval by a judge or magistrate.

In response, the Founding Fathers adopted the Fourth Amendment. This amendment generally requires that the police obtain a warrant from a judge before conducting a search and seizure.

The warrant must explain why the police believe a search is necessary. The warrant must also state what material is being targeted in the search. The British would often use so-called "general warrants" when searching colonists' property. A general warrant allowed authorities to search all of a person's property. The Fourth Amendment generally forbids the use of general warrants. It requires the police to state specifically what items they expect to find.

In order to obtain a warrant and search a person, the police must have what is known as "probable cause." Probable cause means more than just a hunch. The police must point to specified evidence showing that the person likely possesses certain material.

Controversy surrounds the Fourth Amendment because sometimes the police will violate the rights of a person who is carrying contraband, such as illegal drugs. A common example is when a police officer discovers drugs on a person—but only after an unreasonable search or seizure.

Our Constitution allows a person illegally searched to file a motion to suppress the evidence. This is called the exclusionary rule. Judge Benjamin Cardozo expressed this concept when he said, "the criminal is free to go because the constable has blundered."[14] The rationale behind the exclusionary rule is to require law enforcement officials to obey the law.

Public school students do not possess the same level of Fourth Amendment rights as adults in their homes. In 1985, the United States Supreme Court limited the level of Fourth Amendment protection for students.[15] Normally, police must have probable cause to search a person and their belongings. However, the High Court determined that "the school setting requires some easing of the restrictions to which searches by public authorities are ordinarily subject." In that case, the Court found that it was reasonable to search a student's purse after a teacher discovered two girls smoking in the bathroom.[16]

During recent time, the courts have examined numerous Fourth Amendment cases involving the searching of people who are suspected of trafficking in drugs. The epidemic of illegal drug use has led some courts to relax the standards of the Fourth Amendment.

However, the Supreme Court in 2001 ruled unconstitutional a South Carolina state hospital's practice of drug testing pregnant women and then turning positive results over to the police for prosecution. The hospital argued that its program was justified because there is a special need to stop drug use. The majority of the Supreme Court disagreed, finding that the policy violated the Fourth Amendment rights of the pregnant women.[17]

Fourth Amendment rights are fragile because some people are not willing to protect the constitutional rights of those whom they feel have committed crimes.

The Fifth Amendment

> No person shall be held to answer for a capital, or otherwise infamous crime, unless on a presentment or indictment of a Grand Jury, except in cases arising in the land or naval forces, or in the Militia, when in actual service in time of War or public danger; nor shall any person be subject for the same offence to be twice put in jeopardy of life or limb; nor shall be compelled in any criminal case to be a witness against himself, nor be deprived of life, liberty, or property without due process of law; nor shall private property be taken for public use without just compensation.

The Fifth Amendment provides protections for criminal defendants and the general public in several provisions. The freedoms in the Fifth Amendment include the right to be charged with a serious crime by a grand jury, protection against double jeopardy, the right to remain silent, the right of due process and the right to not have property taken by the government without just compensation.

Grand Jury

A grand jury consists of a group of everyday citizens who hear a prosecutor's evidence in a secret proceeding. The grand jury then determines whether there is sufficient evidence to indict or present charges against someone. This group of persons is known as a grand jury, because there are more people in this body than in the ordinary trial jury, or petit jury.

The right to a grand jury serves to protect citizens from aggressive prosecutors. The theory is that an individual's peers will make sure that there is a valid basis for the criminal charges. During colonial times, grand jurors would often refuse to indict fellow colonists for trumped-up charges by British authorities.[18]

Double Jeopardy

Protection from double jeopardy ensures that a person cannot be prosecuted for the same crime more than once. If a jury acquits a criminal defendant of charges, a prosecutor cannot try again with a different jury. The principle dates back to early legal systems, such as Roman law.[19]

There are exceptions to the safeguard against double jeopardy. A person can be charged in separate criminal and civil trials. For example, former football star O. J. Simpson faced criminal murder charges for the 1994 deaths of his ex-wife Nicole Brown Simpson and her companion Ronald Goldman. A jury found Simpson not guilty of the charges. After the completion of the criminal case, the victims' families sued Simpson in civil court for damages and won.

In a criminal case, the state brings charges against an individual to punish that person with fines or confinement.

In a civil suit, normally one private party sues another private party for money. Another exception, shown by the trial of four Los Angeles Police Department officers for beating motorist Rodney King, is that a criminal defendant can sometimes be charged criminally in state court and then in federal court. The officers were charged with different crimes. In state court they faced assault charges. In federal court they faced civil rights charges. This is not double jeopardy because the state and federal governments are separate sovereigns.

The Right to Remain Silent

One of the more important rights contained in the Fifth Amendment is the privilege against self-incrimination, or the right to remain silent. This right means that the state has the burden of proving that a person committed a crime. In court, the criminal defendant does not have to testify. He or she can say: "I take the Fifth."

In a criminal trial, the defendant faces the loss of his or her freedom. Because the burden facing the individual is so great, our Constitution demands that the government prove that the person committed the crime on the basis of evidence rather than force it from the individual it seeks to punish.

The United States Supreme Court has extended the privilege against self-incrimination, or right to remain silent, to outside the courtroom settings.

When a police officer arrests a suspect, the officer is supposed to read the suspect his or her rights. The officer warns the suspect: "You have the right to remain silent. Anything you say can and will be used against you."

The United States Supreme Court in its 1966 decision *Miranda v. Arizona* set up certain procedural safeguards to ensure that suspects retain the constitutional right to remain silent while in police custody. The Court wrote that in the past some law enforcement officials used physical or psychological coercion to obtain confessions. In the lead case, the Court voided the conviction of a young Latino man in part because the police had not informed him of his right to remain silent while they kept him in custody.[20]

"Despite the scorn that has been heaped upon it, the privilege against self-incrimination seems neither irrational nor silly when viewed objectively," writes attorney/author Alfred Knight. "Its essence is a citizen, arms folded, confronting the state and saying, 'Prove it.'"[21]

The Right to Due Process

Due process is one of the greatest rights Americans possess. One legal historian has said the right of due process has "served as the basis for the constitutional protection of the rights of Americans."[22] Due process has often been divided into two basic categories: procedural due process and substantive due process.

Procedural due process means that the government must guarantee a fair process before taking away an individual's life, liberty, or property. The basic elements to procedural due process are notice and the right to a fair hearing. This prevents the government from arbitrarily taking away someone's job or freedom.

The protection of due process is written into both the Fifth Amendment and Fourteenth Amendment. The Fourteenth Amendment applies to the states and extends many of the protections of the Bill of Rights to the states.

The United States Supreme Court determined that Ohio public school officials violated the procedural due-process rights of several public school students by suspending them from school for ten days without prior notice and a hearing. "The Clause requires at least these rudimentary precautions against unfair or mistaken findings of misconduct and arbitrary exclusion from school," the Court wrote.[23]

Substantive due process means that laws must advance a legitimate governmental objective—such as protecting children. Normally, a law must be justified on a rational basis, which means it must be reasonably related to a legitimate goal.

In 1977, the United States Supreme Court struck down a Cleveland, Ohio, zoning law that limited an extended family from living together. A grandmother occupied a house with one of her sons and two of her grandsons. The city had sent the grandmother a notice saying that one of her grandsons was an "illegal occupant" because the grandson was not the child of the son at the house.[24]

When the grandmother refused to comply with the order, the city brought criminal charges against the elderly woman. The Supreme Court determined that the law violated the right to substantive due process. The Court wrote that "the Constitution prevents East Cleveland from standardizing its children and its adults by forcing all to live in certain narrowly defined family patterns."[25]

Right to Just Compensation

The last clause of the Fifth Amendment, called the takings clause, reads "nor shall private property be taken for public use without just compensation." This means that the government cannot simply take a citizen's property without paying for it.

The government does possess the power of eminent domain, or the right to take private property for public use. For example, the government sometimes takes land to build highways. However, the due process clause of the Fifth and Fourteenth Amendments requires that the government give "just compensation" before invoking this sovereign power.

In 1987, the United States Supreme Court ruled that California coastal officials violated the due-process rights of the owners of a beach home.[26] James and Marilyn Nollan sought a permit to rebuild their home on the beachfront property. The officials would grant the permit only if the Nollans granted public access to certain portions of their land.

The Court concluded that the actions were so unfair as to violate due process. If the government "wants an easement across the Nollans' property, it must pay for it."[27]

Sixth Amendment

> In all criminal prosecutions, the accused shall enjoy the right to a speedy and public trial, by an impartial jury of the State and district wherein the crime shall have been committed; which district shall have been previously ascertained by law, and to be informed of the nature and cause of the accusation; to be confronted with the witnesses against him; to have compulsory process for obtaining witnesses in his favor, and to have the assistance of counsel for his defence.

Similar to the Fifth Amendment, the Sixth Amendment provides numerous protections to persons accused of crimes. Most fundamentally, the Sixth Amendment ensures that criminal defendants receive fair trials. The amendment attempts to provide a fair trial by guaranteeing numerous rights.

The Sixth Amendment requires that criminal defendants receive a speedy and public trial before an impartial jury. It also provides that criminal defendants receive proper notice of the charges they are facing. The amendment also provides that criminal defendants can confront their accusers and compel certain witnesses to testify. It provides that criminal defendants have a constitutional right to an attorney.

The right to a speedy trial ensures that a criminal defendant will not sit in jail for too long before having a trial. A public trial ensures that an individual will not be subject to the closed-door justice of the infamous Star Chamber in England.

The Star Chamber was an English court dissolved by Parliament in 1641, which was known for its secretive judicial meetings and harsh sentences. It would convict and punish individuals without providing them with any protections comparable to those found in our Bill of Rights.

An impartial jury must also judge every person charged with a crime. Sometimes, a judge will pick a jury from another county than the one in which the defendant allegedly committed the crime. In our legal system, this is called a change of venue.

Judges consider changing venue when they believe that a defendant could not receive a fair trial in the city or county where the alleged crime took place. This potential problem occurs when a high-profile criminal case receives a lot of pretrial publicity. Judges have a duty to ensure that a defendant will not be prejudged by the jury.

The Sixth Amendment also provides that a defendant must have notice of the charges filed against him. Individuals need to know what charges they face so that they can prepare a defense. The next clause of the amendment, called the confrontation clause, ensures that a criminal defendant can cross-examine those who testify against him. United States Supreme Court Justice Antonin Scalia has written: "The perception that confrontation is essential to fairness has persisted over the centuries because there is much truth to it. . . . It is always more difficult to tell a lie about a person 'to his face' than 'behind his back.'"[28]

The Sixth Amendment also provides that a criminal defendant can force witnesses to testify in the trial. Often, people do not want to get involved in a criminal trial. The compulsory witness clause provides that a defendant can try to prove his or her case whether the witnesses want to get involved or not.

Finally, the Sixth Amendment ensures that a criminal defendant can have a defense attorney. In 1963, the United States Supreme Court ruled that a criminal defendant charged with any felony had the right to counsel even if he or she could not afford an attorney.[29] That decision led to the establishment of public defender offices in the federal and state court systems. Public defenders represent people charged with state or federal crimes who do not have the money to pay for their own attorney.

The Seventh Amendment

> In Suits at common law, where the value in controversy shall exceed twenty dollars, the right of trial by jury shall be preserved, and no fact tried by a jury, shall be otherwise re-examined in any Court of the United States, than according to the rules of the common law.

The Sixth Amendment provides a jury trial to a criminal defendant. The Seventh Amendment extends this right of jury trial to federal civil cases. Employees who sue their employers in federal court for discrimination can have their case heard by a jury. The Seventh Amendment safeguards the right of a person in a federal civil suit to have his or her case heard by a jury of peers. In our legal system, the jury decides questions of fact, while the judge decides questions of law.

This does not mean that anytime one person or business sues another in federal court, the lawsuit will go before a jury. Many cases never reach a jury because the parties settle their dispute or the judge dismisses the case, finding there are no material factual disputes.

The Eighth Amendment

> Excessive bail shall not be required, nor excessive fines
> imposed, nor cruel and unusual punishment inflicted.

The English 1689 Bill of Rights also contained a provision prohibiting excessive bail and fines and cruel and
unusual punishment. Several states contained provisions
in their constitutions that established that penalties
should be proportional to the charged offense.

The Eighth Amendment was added to the Bill of
Rights to protect people from being locked up in jail
because they could not pay costly fines. In England, some
defendants were financially burdened on trumped-up
charges and could not pay the fines to get out of jail. For
example, in 1631, Puritan clergyman Alexander Leighton
was fined ten thousand pounds for libeling the leaders of
the Anglican Church, the country's official church.[30]

The most controversial aspect of the Eighth
Amendment is the "cruel and unusual punishment"
clause. The question that continues to divide citizens of
our country is whether the death penalty constitutes cruel
and unusual punishment.

In 1972, the United States Supreme Court ruled 5–4
in *Furman* v. *Georgia* that state laws giving juries unlimited
discretion in the administration of the death penalty were
unconstitutional.[31] The majority of the court reasoned that
the state failed to provide sufficient guidelines for a jury in
death-penalty cases. The court said that the decision
whether or not to impose a sentence of death was too arbitrary. This decision led to the suspension of all executions
in the United States for several years.

Many state legislatures amended their death penalty laws
to give more guidance to judges and juries in capital cases.
Several of these new laws were challenged and in 1976, the
United States Supreme Court ruled in *Gregg* v. *Georgia* that

the death penalty itself does not violate the Constitution.[32] The majority of the Court reasoned that the state of Georgia had changed its statute to give juries enough guidance that death sentences would not be arbitrary.

Today, close to one hundred inmates are executed each year.

The Ninth Amendment

> The enumeration in the Constitution of certain rights shall not be construed to deny or disparage others retained by the people.

One common objection to the Bill of Rights when it was first considered was that listing, or enumerating, certain rights would mean that those were the only rights the people possessed.

To answer this concern, Congress adopted the Ninth Amendment. It implies that people retain other rights not specifically listed in the Bill of Rights. Historian Leonard Levy writes that "the Ninth Amendment could also serve to draw the sting from any criticism that the catalog of personal freedoms was incomplete."[33]

For 175 years, the Ninth Amendment "lay dormant" and was a "constitutional curiosity."[34] In 1965, the United States Supreme Court ruled that the Ninth Amendment provided a right of marital privacy. In *Griswold* v. *Connecticut*, the Supreme Court struck down a Connecticut law prohibiting the use of contraceptives.[35]

The Tenth Amendment

> The powers not delegated to the United States by the Constitution, nor prohibited by it to the States, are reserved to the States respectively, or to the people.

The Anti-Federalists, a political party opposed to a strong central government, opposed the Constitution because they feared a federal government could swallow up the rights of states and individuals. Those who think the federal government is invading the authority of state officials will cite the Tenth Amendment and "states' rights."

Before and during the Civil War and the civil rights movement, some Southern politicians committed to slavery and segregation claimed the federal government was infringing on states' rights. These officials argued that it was up to state officials to determine the policies of the state.

Recently, challenges to several federal gun control laws have been argued on Tenth Amendment grounds. The argument advanced by the opponents of the laws is that the states, not the federal government, should regulate the sale of handguns.

A Difficult Process to Individual Freedom

The freedoms in the Bill of Rights are second nature to many Americans. Nearly all citizens realize that the Constitution gives us the right to free speech and the right to be free from unreasonable searches and seizures.

However, the development of the Bill of Rights was not an easy process. No other country has a Constitution and Bill of Rights that safeguards personal liberty to the extent our country does. In the next few chapters, we will see the historical background of the Bill of Rights and the difficult political battle that led to the Constitution and the Bill of Rights.

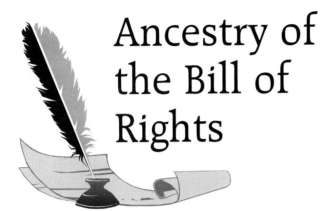

2

Ancestry of the Bill of Rights

As great as the Founding Fathers were, they did not create the Bill of Rights out of a vacuum. Our leaders were greatly influenced by other great documents in English and colonial history.

It should come as no surprise that the roots of American law and several concepts of the Bill of Rights came from England. One legal scholar writes that "the slightly embarrassing fact was that the liberties Congress proposed in 1789 had mostly been created and defined by America's great oppressor, England."[1]

Most of the colonists came from England, many fleeing to the new land in pursuit of religious and personal freedom.

Magna Carta

Many historians trace the origins of the Bill of Rights to the great English document known as Magna Carta. This Latin phrase means great charter. Attorney and author Al Knight writes: "This charter is the source of many of the provisions of the American Bill of Rights, which were adopted more than five hundred years later in a more civilized environment."[2]

In the early thirteenth century, many barons, or leading noblemen in England were upset with the actions of King John. They felt the king was exerting too much power and not respecting their rights. In June 1215, King John was forced to recognize that the nobility and freemen of England were entitled to certain rights. These rights were set down in the Magna Carta. The document was not a ringing endorsement for equality. It was designed only to provide protection for certain feudal lords. Nevertheless, it remains an important source for the American Bill of Rights.

A few provisions in the Magna Carta remain important today. The most cited provision of the document is Chapter 39, which declares: "No free man shall be captured or imprisoned or disseised or outlawed or exiled or in any way destroyed . . . except by the lawful judgment of his peers and by the law of the land." The key parts of this phrase are "by the lawful judgment of his peers" and "by the law of the land." These phrases are early expressions of what would later become trial by jury and due process of law.

The most important principle of the document was that the king had to obey and was not above the law.

Petition of Right

The kings of England acted arbitrarily, ignoring the spirit of the Magna Carta. When Charles I took the throne in 1625, he acted without regard to the rights of his subjects. He imprisoned people for refusing to pay him monies. He also forced people to house troops in their homes.

Believing the actions of the king to be unreasonable and unlawful, Sir Edward Coke, a former jurist and well-known writer, called on his fellow members of Parliament to respond to the king's abuses. Parliament passed a declaration known as the Petition of Right of 1628.

This document provided that Parliament, the English legislative body, had to consent to taxes. It also barred the king from forcing people to house troops in their homes.

Though the Petition does serve as an antecedent for the English Bill of Rights and the United States Bill of Rights, it did not fulfill its promise. Charles continued to violate civil liberties throughout his reign, which ended in civil war and his execution in 1649.

English Bill of Rights of 1689

The Petition of Right did not solve the power struggle between the monarchy and the Parliament. Charles' son, Charles II, took the throne in 1660. After Charles II died, his brother King James II became king.

The power struggle between the king and many of his subjects continued. In 1688, James II was forced to leave England. Parliament revolted against the king's attempts at grasping power. When King William and Queen Mary assumed power under the Glorious Revolution of 1688, they took the throne on the condition imposed by Parliament that they abide by a statute that came to be known as the English Bill of Rights of 1689.

The document established that no king of England could dominate Parliament as Charles I and James II tried to do. It increased the power of Parliament and declared that its members could speak and debate freely without fear of retribution by the monarchy.[3]

One provision in the English Bill of Rights provides that "excessive bail ought not to be required, nor excessive fines imposed, nor cruel and unusual punishments inflicted." This provision served as the model for the Eighth Amendment. Another provision provided for the right to bear arms.

The English Bill of Rights did not provide as much protection as the United States Bill of Rights. The English Bill of Rights could be changed by Parliament. It was designed to increase the power of Parliament and reduce the power of the king. However, the English Bill of Rights served as an important foundation for the U.S. Bill of Rights. It expanded on the notion first expressed in the Magna Carta that the government must obey the rule of law.

Colonial Charters and Laws

Many people fled England to the New World to escape religious persecution. For centuries, conflict between Protestants and Roman Catholics led to disruption and even bloodshed.

These colonists set up governments that contain provisions for basic human liberty. In 1639, the Maryland General Assembly approved the Act for the Liberties of the People. Scholar Bernard Schwartz says that this basic document "may be considered the first American bill of rights."[4]

A provision in the Maryland law provides that a colonist or his property cannot be infringed upon except "according to the Laws of this province." The colonies set up charters headed by a royal governor who still answered to the King of England. This provision provides an "American link" between the Magna Carta and the due process clause of the U.S. Constitution.[5]

In 1641, the leaders of the Massachusetts colony passed the Massachusetts Body of Liberties. This provision served as the model for later colonial charters in both New York and Pennsylvania. The document contained provisions allowing for freedom of speech at public meetings, the right to counsel, jury trials, and freedom from cruel and unusual punishment.

However, the Puritans of Massachusetts did require

residents of the colony to conform to their religious faiths. Those who disagreed with the Puritan leaders were declared dissidents and some were banished from the colony. One religious leader banished from the Massachusetts colony was Roger Williams. Williams was a true pioneer of religious freedom. He believed that church and state should remain separate or else religious persecution would result.

Williams founded the colony of Rhode Island. In 1663, he ensured that the colony's charter would provide religious freedom to the colonists. Schwartz writes that "the Rhode Island charter was the first to contain a grant of religious freedom in the all-inclusive terms that are familiar in American constitutions."[6]

Though the colonial charters provided protection to colonists, they pale in comparison to the protections of our Bill of Rights. Colonial charters could be changed much more easily than the United States Constitution. Also, the colonies were still subject to the whims of the English king and Parliament. Colonial leaders enjoyed a good deal of self-government. They gradually became more assertive of their rights with respect to the far-away English crown.

The colonists would eventually break free of the crown after the Declaration of Independence and the Revolutionary War, or the War of Independence.

Revolutionary Documents

In the beginning, most colonists were loyal to England. The English government was more concerned with France and Spain regarding control over the New World than it was in controlling its colonists.

In 1763, England had prevailed over France in the Seven Years' War in North America. The war is also known as the French and Indian War. After winning this war, the English government focused more attention on its American colonies.

England was a leading world power with an international empire. It needed substantial revenues to operate this empire. The Seven Years' War had depleted much of its revenue. The colonies proved to be a vital source of income for the British empire.

In the meantime, colonial leaders began to see themselves as independent and grew more ambitious. Historian Howard Zinn writes: "So, the American leadership was less in need of English rule, the English more in need of the colonists' wealth. The elements were there for conflict."[7]

This time of conflict led to the creation of American law. King George III and Parliament imposed a variety of measures designed to tax the colonists to raise revenue for the crown. These included the Stamp Act of 1765 and the Tea Act of 1773.

After the uprising known as the Boston Tea Party, the British government responded with the Coercion, or Intolerable, Acts, which closed the Boston harbor for trading. These measures essentially dissolved the colonial government.

These experiences caused colonial leaders, such as Thomas Jefferson and Thomas Paine, to revolt against injustice. Paine wrote a pamphlet entitled *Common Sense* that was widely read and wildly popular. It expressed the idea of revolting against England.

American colonists believed King George III was treating them unjustly with the taxes he and his Parliament levied on Americans.

In 1775, the tensions between the colonists and the British escalated into war. While the war was being fought, Richard Henry Lee of Virginia introduced a measure in the Continental Congress on June 7, 1776, calling for a revolutionary declaration of independence. The Continental Congress was made up of a group of colonial leaders and foreshadowed America's future independent government.

Lee's call led to Jefferson's drafting of the famous revolutionary declaration in American history—the Declaration of Independence.

Declaration of Independence

The Declaration of Independence was the blueprint and justification for the colonists' uprising and the Revolutionary War. It established a moral authority against the unjust and arbitrary laws of King George III. Though the Declaration of Independence is not a bill of rights, it protested the king's violation of several basic rights, including: trial by a jury of one's peers and quartering of royalist troops in colonists' homes. The document cited numerous abuses of George III, the King of England, and declared him a tyrant. It accused the king of "quartering large Bodies of Armed Troops among us" and "obstructed the Administration of Justice."

The Continental Congress officially proclaimed the document on July 4, 1776, which is why July 4 is known as Independence Day.

Perhaps the most well-known phrase of the document is the provision about certain "self-evident" principles. The document read: "all Men are created equal, that they are endowed by their Creator with certain unalienable Rights . . . Life, Liberty, and the Pursuit of Happiness." Unfortunately, the lofty language of the Declaration of Independence did not include African Americans or

The Declaration of Independence not only proclaimed that the American colonies were breaking free from England, but spelled out some of the political beliefs of the Founding Fathers, such as the idea that "all men are created equal."

women. Historian Howard Zinn writes: "It was just that women were beyond consideration as worthy of inclusion. They were politically invisible."[8]

By the time of the Declaration of Independence, many colonists believed strongly that a government must operate according to certain fundamental laws. However, many colonists still supported the British government, or at least did not want to totally separate themselves from it. Many were not in favor of war.

Colonial leaders believed they were fit to govern themselves under their own forms of government. In May 1776, the Second Continental Congress issued a resolution calling for each colony to establish its own government. Patriot and future second President John Adams referred to this call for action as "the most important Resolution that was ever taken in America."[9]

This resolution urged the colonists to draft constitutions that would provide protections for individual liberties. Rights protected in a constitution were far more powerful and long-lasting than rights granted in a colonial charter or even measures passed by a legislative body.

Virginia Declaration of Rights

Virginia responded to the Second Continental Congress' call for new government with a constitution and a declaration of rights. The Virginia Declaration of Rights protected many of the same individual freedoms as the Bill of Rights.

The Virginia Declaration of Rights contained articles protecting the right to free exercise of religion, a free press, right to be free from unreasonable searches and seizures, the right against self-incrimination, due process, just compensation, speedy trial, jury trial, the right to confront one's accusers, freedom from cruel and unusual punishment, and the right to a jury trial in civil cases.

George Mason, the author of the Virginia Declaration of Rights, was one of the strongest advocates of a federal bill of rights.

George Mason, a planter without formal legal training, drew up the document. His creation served as a model for eight of twelve other states that formed new constitutions during the revolutionary era.

How the Constitution and the Bill of Rights Developed

The colonists began setting up their own governments during the revolutionary period. Each colony drafted its own constitution to govern its people. The system of government was state-centered. The English experience had convinced American leaders that a strong central government was dangerous. For this reason, our early leaders wanted to create a limited national government.

The colonies eventually prevailed in the Revolutionary War after General George Washington defeated Lord Cornwallis in the Battle of Yorktown in 1781. That year, the colonies formed a central government under the Articles of Confederation. Though the Articles of Confederation were designed to bind the thirteen states into a union, the result was anything but successful. The Articles of Confederation failed because it did not give enough power to Congress to govern the different states effectively.

The states fought over trade and commerce issues, boundaries, and the creation of new states in the western territories. The Articles of Confederation created a weak government that was unable to raise revenue, raise troops, regulate commerce, settle disputes between different states and enforce its own laws.

Under the Articles of Confederation, the Congress could not force state governments to raise monies for the federal government. This was a problem particularly because of the large amount of war debt.

Leaders in various states began to see the need for a stronger national government. Revolutionary war hero and future first president George Washington saw the need for a strong central government firsthand after his troops lacked funds for basic supplies during the Revolutionary War.

In July 1785, the Massachusetts legislature passed a measure calling for amendments to the Articles of Confederation. Other states also began to recognize the problems associated with a weak central government. However, many states refused to make the necessary changes because it would mean a loss of state sovereignty.

In March 1785, representatives from Maryland, Virginia, and later Pennsylvania met at George Washington's Virginia estate, Mount Vernon, to discuss

thorny issues involving fishing and navigation rights along the Potomac River. The conference showed that individual states could work together in pursuit of the common good.

George Washington hosted representatives from different states at his home in Virginia. There, some prominent politicians began to discuss the need to revise the Articles of Confederation.

The Mount Vernon meeting led to the so-called Annapolis Convention in September 1786. At this meeting, delegates from five states discussed interstate commercial and trade issues. Concerned that only five states sent representatives, the leaders at the Annapolis meeting adopted a resolution. It called for representatives from all thirteen states to meet at Philadelphia the next May to discuss changes to the Articles of Confederation.[1] New York political leader Alexander Hamilton, a proponent of a strong central government, drafted a letter to the various states calling for the meeting that would discuss political, as well as commercial, issues.

While leaders from different states were meeting, other events showed the real need for a strong central government. In 1786, an uprising of farmers in Massachusetts called Shays' Rebellion convinced many other leaders of the need for a strong national government.

Daniel Shays was a Revolutionary War veteran. After the war, he and many other farmers found themselves hauled into court for debts. Many of the farmers were outraged because the debts grew while they were fighting in the war. Shays organized over one thousand farmers and marched on courthouses in Springfield and Boston.

Though a state militia funded by wealthy Boston

Daniel Shays and his fellow indebted farmers staged a revolt in 1786–1787 that would underline the need for a stronger federal government.

merchants dispersed the angry farmers, Shays' Rebellion showed the need for a strong central government.

Congress endorsed the movement to revise the Articles of Confederation in February 1787. Congress did not, however, endorse the drafting of an entirely new Constitution, but that is what happened.

Philadelphia Convention

The Founding Fathers, or Framers, created the United States Constitution at the Philadelphia Convention. Though seventy-four delegates were named to the convention, only fifty-five showed up in Philadelphia to establish a better form of government, or, in the words of the resulting document, "a more perfect union."

The effort of the fifty-five delegates in creating the Constitution has been called the "Miracle at Philadelphia." The delegates focused upon creating a stronger, more functional central government. The delegates were not concerned with individual rights, such as freedom of speech, but with governmental "functions and interests."[2]

The primary intent of James Madison and his fellow members of the convention was to create a strong central government. As one scholar writes, "the original intent of the Founding Fathers was to have no bill of rights at all."[3] Towards the end of the Constitutional Convention in September, George Mason, the author of the Virginia Declaration of Rights, proposed the idea of a bill of rights. Mason said: "I wish that a bill of rights had been included in the preface to the plan. It would be a great quiet to the people."

A motion by Eldridge Gerry and Mason to include a bill of rights was soundly rejected. Attorney and author Al Knight writes: "In its historic debut, the American Magna Charta was dead on arrival."[4] Many Founding Fathers apparently believed that a bill of rights was unnecessary either because individual rights were provided for in state constitutions or in the Constitution as it was written. "No delegate had been against such rights," writes historian Catherine Drinker Bowen. "Merely, they considered the Constitution covered the matter as it stood."[5]

Most leaders at the Philadelphia Convention believed that a Bill of Rights was unnecessary, useless, and maybe even dangerous. Other Framers may simply have wanted to go home after months of deliberation.[6] Some argued that the addition of a bill of rights was dangerous because it might imply that the government had greater power than it actually had. The argument was that the listing of certain rights would imply that no other rights existed. A bill of rights would expressly limit the federal government's power. Some thought it would imply that the government had all powers that were not expressly limited.

After the Philadelphia Convention, Richard Henry Lee of Virginia made a motion in the Confederation Congress to add a bill of rights to the Constitution before submitting it to the states for ratification. The Confederation Congress rejected Lee's motion.

Ratification of the U.S. Constitution

On September 17, 1787, thirty-nine delegates at the Constitutional Convention in Philadelphia signed the Constitution. The Constitution contains seven sections called articles. Article VII provides: "The ratification of the conventions of nine states shall be sufficient for the establishment of the Constitution between the states so ratifying the same." This meant that nine states had to approve the Constitution.

Ratification, or official approval, was not an easy process. Political leaders were divided on the issue. Supporters of the new Constitution with its strong central government called themselves Federalists. Opponents of the Constitution were known as Anti-Federalists. Many of the Anti-Federalists opposed the Constitution because it failed to provide for a bill of rights. They also believed it gave too much power to the federal government at the expense of the state governments.

On Sept. 28, 1787, the Congress directed the state legislatures to set up ratification conventions to approve the new document. Many Anti-Federalists argued the members of the Philadelphia Convention had exceeded their authority in creating this bold new document.

The Anti-Federalists were particularly concerned with the so-called "necessary and proper" clause of the new Constitution. Article I, Section 1, clause 8 provided Congress with the power to "make all Laws which shall be necessary and proper" for executing its powers vested in the Constitution. The Anti-Federalists believed this clause gave Congress the power to do what it wanted.

In the key, populous states of New York and Virginia, the Anti-Federalists fought a hard political battle over ratification.

After the Philadelphia Convention, James Madison co-wrote a series of anonymous articles in support of the Constitution with Alexander Hamilton and John Jay. These 85 essays, known as *The Federalist Papers*, appeared as newspaper articles in New York. They are considered the

Financial genius Alexander Hamilton was one of the three authors of The Federalist Papers, *a series of essays designed to win support for the new Constitution.*

definitive work on the Constitution. Thomas Jefferson once called them "the best commentary on the principles of government which ever was written."[7]

These articles discussed the framework of the Constitution, including the principles of checks and balances and separation of powers among three branches of government.

The battle between the Federalists and Anti-Federalists was intense. However, the Federalists possessed several advantages. First, their selection of the name "Federalist" was important for their campaign. It left their opponents with the "weak and negative label 'Anti-Federalists.'"[8]

The Federalists also enjoyed most of the media support, as the large newspapers from Boston, New York, and Philadelphia took up the Federalist cause.[9] Finally, the Federalists seemed to have the best ammunition—the detailed document known as the Constitution. The Federalists argued the benefits of the document, while the Anti-Federalists could only criticize it.[10]

Delaware became the first state to ratify the Constitution on December 7, 1787. It did so unanimously. Pennsylvania ratified the Constitution a few days later on December 12. The delegates voted 46 to 23 in favor of the Constitution.

The Pennsylvania delegates also considered fifteen amendments proposed by Anti-Federalist Robert Whitehill. These proposed amendments were similar to what would later become the Bill of Rights.[11]

The delegates voted against the amendments by the same two to one margin. The Anti-Federalists then issued "The Address and Reasons of Dissent of the Minority of the Convention." This document spelled out the need for individual liberties and spread the push for a bill of rights.[12]

New Jersey ratified the Constitution unanimously on

December 18, 1787. Georgia also ratified it unanimously on January 2, 1788.

However, the ratification of the Constitution faced a tremendous struggle in several of the more populous states, including Massachusetts and New York. On February 6, 1788, Massachusetts voted 187 to 168 in favor of the Constitution only after the Federalists agreed to recommend amending the Constitution to include protections for individual liberties. Massachusetts became the first state to officially recommend amendments to the Constitution during the ratification process. Though the nine amendments bear little resemblance to the final Bill of Rights, their importance lies in the fact that Massachusetts started a pattern of attaching amendments.[13] Even though the amendments were only a recommendation, it helped pave the way for the later addition of the Bill of Rights.

New Hampshire became the required ninth state on June 21, 1788, voting 57 to 46 in favor of the Constitution. Although the Constitution was technically in effect after New Hampshire ratified it, the Framers needed the support of Virginia to have an effective new government.

Virginia was the home of James Madison, George Washington, and Thomas Jefferson—all of whom supported the Constitution. However, the state was also the home of a group of well-known Anti-Federalists, including Patrick Henry and George Mason.

On June 25, 1788, James Madison managed to gather enough support for the Constitution in the Virginia state convention. The delegates narrowly approved the Constitution. Two days later, a committee at the Virginia convention proposed that a bill of rights be added to the Constitution.

The Virginia-proposed bill of rights was detailed. Nearly every one of its twenty provisions found a place in the Bill of Rights. After the pro-Constitution victory in Virginia, Congress declared the new Constitution to be the law of the land on July 2, 1788.

The majority of the state ratifying conventions accepted the new Constitution but had recommended adding amendments for individual liberty. However, in several of the states, there was another set of amendments that dealt not with individual liberty issues, but with altering the balance of power between the states and the federal government.

Many of the Anti-Federalists were concerned with the powers of the new Congress to levy direct taxes, maintain a standing army, and to control elections. In other words, many Anti-Federalists opposed the Constitution more because it gave too much power to the federal government than because it failed to include a bill of rights.

The Anti-Federalist position for a bill of rights had great appeal to most people. Most Americans had just fought a bloody revolutionary war for freedom. The Anti-Federalists argued that the people should have their individual liberties protected in the new Constitution. Richard Henry Lee, an Anti-Federalist who refused to serve as a delegate at the Constitutional Convention, wrote *Letters from the Federal Farmer to the Republican.* Lee criticized the new government as undemocratic.

Most of the states had protections for individual

Richard Henry Lee of Virginia was one of the most prominent of the Anti-Federalists.

liberties in their state constitutions. It stood to reason that the people would need these same protections in the federal constitution against a much more powerful central government.

These arguments seemed to sway the general population. There was much opposition to the document because it contained no bill of rights.

Federalist James Madison, who later became known as the Father of the Bill of Rights, understood the difficult and fragile position of the new Constitution. Madison recognized that the addition of a bill of rights would help gain support for the Constitution. However, Madison needed some persuasion to reach this position. This persuasion came from his political mentor and the author of the Declaration of Independence, Thomas Jefferson.

The Father of the Bill of Rights

The leading figure in the adoption of the Bill of Rights was the future fourth President of the United States, James Madison. Though small in stature, this Virginian loomed large in American constitutional history. In fact, he is often called the Father of the Constitution and the Father of the Bill of Rights.

Born and raised in Virginia, Madison attended and graduated from the College of New Jersey (now Princeton University). Through the influence of his father, he became involved in politics in his home state. He was elected to Congress in 1779. He played a vital role in the drafting of the Constitution and the Bill of Rights. He later served as Jefferson's secretary of state. From 1809 to 1871, he served two terms as president of the United States.

Historians and all Americans who are interested in the past owe a huge debt to James Madison. It was he who wrote daily notes on what happened at the Philadelphia Convention. Without these notes, we would know little about the closed-door proceedings.

Americans also owe a great deal to James Madison

James Madison was originally opposed to the idea of including a bill of rights in the Constitution. Eventually, however, he changed his mind and became a champion of the cause.

because it was he who convinced a majority of Congress and his fellow Federalists to amend the Constitution. However, Madison himself originally did not support a bill of rights.

Madison had helped write *The Federalist Papers*, advocating against amending the Constitution. In Federalist No. 84, Alexander Hamilton had argued that bills of rights "are not only unnecessary in the proposed Constitution but would even be dangerous."[1] He argued that a bill of rights was dangerous because it could grant powers to government that it did not possess. Using freedom of the press as an example, Hamilton wrote: "Why, for instance, should it be said that the liberty of the press shall not be restrained, when no power is given by which restrictions may be imposed?"[2]

Hamilton also noted that "the Constitution is itself, in every rational sense, and to every useful purpose, A BILL OF RIGHTS."[3] This view has some merit. The Constitution does provide protection for individual rights. For example, the Constitution prohibits Congress from requiring people to take religious tests to hold federal office.[4]

The Constitution also prohibits *ex post facto* laws and bills of attainder.[5] An *ex post facto* law is a law that punishes someone for conduct that was not a crime at the time the conduct occurred. A bill of attainder is a law that declares a person guilty of a crime and punishes that person without a trial.

James Madison originally subscribed to the view that a bill of rights was unnecessary. He later referred to a bill of rights as a "paper barrier" that would not offer any real protection to the people and may even expand the power of the government.

Madison Hears from Thomas Jefferson

However, another great Founding Father convinced Madison of the importance of the Bill of Rights. This was none other than the future third President of the United States, Thomas Jefferson. Both Jefferson and Madison were leading politicians who both lived in Virginia.

The two engaged in a correspondence across the Atlantic Ocean because Jefferson was serving his country as ambassador to France. Thus, while Madison took a leading role at the Philadelphia Convention, Jefferson could only wait to hear from overseas.

The two men wrote a series of letters about a bill of rights. The correspondence began with Madison's letter of October 24, 1787. Madison informed Jefferson that the legal blueprint that came out of Philadelphia contained no Bill of Rights.

Madison also informed Jefferson that George Mason, the draftsman of the Virginia Declaration of Rights, had opposed the Constitution in part because it did not contain a bill of rights.

Jefferson responded to Madison's doubts from Paris in a letter dated December 20, 1787. He criticized the omission of a bill of rights. Jefferson wrote:

> Let me add that a bill of rights is what the people are entitled to against every government on earth, general or particular, and what no just government should refuse, or rest on inference.[6]

Thomas Jefferson persuaded Madison that the inclusion of a bill of rights was necessary to secure popular support for the new Constitution. Madison wrote to Jefferson in October 1788 that "My own opinion has always been in favor of a bill of rights." However, Madison also wrote in his letter that he believed a bill of rights would be a mere "parchment barrier" that could not protect citizens from an oppressive majority.

Madison believed that the real danger to individual liberty lay not in the government but from what nineteenth century French observer Alexis de Tocqueville called "the tyranny of the majority."[7] Madison feared that, in a democracy, the majority would not respect the rights of the minority.

Madison came to support the inclusion of a bill of rights because he thought it was essential for popular support for the Constitution. Madison believed that the bill of rights would not be very effective in protecting liberties against the will of the majority. In his letter to Jefferson, historians have interpreted that Madison viewed the bill of rights with lukewarm support: "I have favored it [the bill of rights] because I have supposed it might be of use and if properly executed could not be of disservice."

On March 15, 1789, Jefferson responded to Madison's October letter by stressing the importance of a bill of rights. Jefferson disagreed with Madison's assessment about the effectiveness of a bill of rights. Jefferson pointed out that a declaration of rights would provide the judicial branch of government with a "legal check" to ensure the protection of individual rights.

Jefferson warned that omitting a bill of rights would pose a far greater problem than any problems caused by a bill of rights. He wrote: "The inconveniences of the declaration are that it may cramp government in its useful exertions. But the evil of this is shortlived, moderate, and reparable. The inconveniences of the want of a declaration are permanent, afflicting, and irreparable; they are in constant progression from bad to worse."

Jefferson's appeals to Madison transformed the latter from an ambivalent supporter into the man who was later to become known as the "Father of the Bill of Rights."

Madison Becomes Supporter of Bill of Rights

Madison determined that a bill of rights was necessary for two reasons: to establish public opinion in favor of the new Constitution and to guard against the possibility of the abuse of power that is a natural danger with any government.

Madison clearly saw that the general populace greatly desired a bill of rights. The people were mistrustful of the new, powerful central government established by the Constitution.

Historian Robert Goldwin argues that James Madison used the bill of rights to save the Constitution. During the meeting of the First Congress in 1789, some political leaders were calling for a Second Constitutional Convention to amend the Constitution.

Madison feared that these calls would lead to drastic revisions of the Constitution and drastically reduce the power of the federal government. Madison considered this a serious threat to the Constitution.

Opponents of the Constitution were concerned about the power of the new federal government. They were fearful that the federal government would swallow up the power of individual states.

Madison used the public demand for a bill of rights "to thwart [prevent] all efforts to weaken the Constitution."[8] Madison had many proposed amendments to draw upon from the various state conventions. Madison knew he had to propose amendments to the Constitution that he had helped create.

His genius lay in knowing which amendments to introduce and which to exclude. He included provisions protecting individual liberty and left out those amendments that would have taken power away from the federal government. Nearly all of Madison's proposed amendments dealt with issues of individual liberties. He avoided the demand for structural amendments to the Constitution.

Therefore, on June 8, 1789, Madison, a member of the House of Representatives, delivered what one historian has called "one of the most consequential political orations in American history."[9] In his speech in the House, Madison passionately argued for the inclusion of a bill of rights.

Madison told his colleagues that they should consider a bill of rights "in order to quiet that anxiety which prevails in the public mind."[10] Madison said that the inclusion of a bill of rights would show the people that no one wishes "to deprive them of the liberty for which they valiantly fought and honorably bled....You ought not to disregard their inclination, but, on principles of amity and moderation, conform to their wishes and declare the great rights of mankind secured under the Constitution," Madison said.[11]

Amending the Constitution

5

Madison had a tough assignment in persuading the Congress to support a bill of rights. Madison had to clear two high hurdles. First, he had to convince his fellow Federalists that a bill of rights was necessary. Secondly, he had to propose a bill of rights that would not take too much power from the federal government.

Madison had to act quickly. Anti-Federalists from the two major states of New York and Virginia were already urging for a Second Constitutional Convention to discuss amendments to the Constitution. Madison wanted to avoid a second convention, fearing that it would radically change the Constitution.

Madison believed that by carefully selecting amendments dealing with individual liberty, he could take the popular support currently enjoyed by the Anti-Federalists.

Fortunately for Madison, he had an advantage: the makeup of the Congress. The First Congress was overwhelmingly Federalist. There were only ten Anti-Federalists in the House and two in the Senate. This ensured the defeat of the Anti-Federalist amendments.

However, he still had to convince a majority of his fellow Federalists about the need for a bill of rights. This was no small task. Many Federalists had adopted a position similar to that expressed by Alexander Hamilton, who opposed a bill of rights.

Madison's Amendments

In his June 8, 1789, speech, Madison appealed to his fellow Federalists, saying that the adoption of a bill of rights would cause the people "to join their support to the cause of federalism, if they were satisfied on this one point."[1]

Madison recognized that many of his fellow congressmen and Federalists were against amending the Constitution they had worked so hard to craft.

Madison recognized the arguments against a bill of rights. He even remarked that "these arguments are not entirely without foundation."[2] However, Madison repeatedly emphasized the favorable reaction of the public to adding a bill of rights.

He added that "if there was reason for restraining the state governments from exercising this power, there is like reason for restraining the federal government."[3] Madison also noted that the different rights mentioned in the state bills of rights were different and some were "defective."[4]

Madison concluded that the addition of a bill of rights "will be proper" and "highly politic, for the tranquility of the public mind and the stability of the government."[5]

Madison's Proposed Amendments

After addressing the arguments, Madison then introduced his particular provisions. He proposed nine amendments as the Bill of Rights.

The first amendment would be added to the beginning of the Constitution and would declare that "all power is originally vested in, and consequently derived from, the people." His other proposed amendments would be added to the text of the Constitution.

Amendment two dealt with the number of representatives per population and the third amendment dealt with congressional pay raises.

Madison's original amendment four contained provisions for religious freedom, free speech, right to bear arms, due process, and freedom from cruel and unusual punishment. Madison's fifth amendment provided: "no state shall violate the equal rights of conscience, or freedom of the press, or trial by jury in criminal cases." This proposal would have protected individuals from state governments.

His sixth amendment dealt with appeals to the United States Supreme Court. The seventh amendment provided for unanimous jury verdicts in criminal cases. His eighth amendment said each branch of government could not exercise powers of the other branch. Madison's ninth amendment merely renumbered articles of the Constitution.

Even though the style and form was different, the substance of Madison's original amendments survived in the Bill of Rights. Madison took his proposed amendments from the various suggestions of the states at their ratifying conventions.

Some members of Congress immediately opposed Madison's idea. For example, Representative James Jackson from Georgia, a Federalist, echoed an argument from Hamilton's Federalist No. 84. He argued that listing certain rights of the people, would imply greater powers to the government. He reasoned that "those [powers] omitted are inferred to be resigned to the discretion of the government."[6]

Another representative, Anti-Federalist Elbridge Gerry from Massachusetts argued that there were simply more important matters for the Congress to consider than

Elbridge Gerry of Massachusetts was a strong Anti-Federalist. Once the Constitution was in place, however, he believed the government had more important matters to consider than the addition of a bill of rights.

the bill of rights. Gerry believed the government needed to tend to the day-to-day operations of the country. He said that "the great wheels of the political machine should first be set in motion . . . lest she lays by the wharf till she beats off her rudder, and runs herself a wreck on shore."[7]

Despite these powerful arguments, Madison was able to prevail in his quest for a bill of rights. In July 1789, a House Select Committee approved of Madison's amendments in virtually the same form as Madison had proposed.

Representative Roger Sherman proposed on August 13 that the amendments be placed at the end of the Constitution. "We ought not to interweave our propositions into the work itself, because it will be destructive of the whole fabric," he said. "The constitution is the act of the people and ought to remain entire."[8]

Madison responded that there was a "neatness" to adding the amendments to the body of the Constitution, but ever the diplomat he conceded, saying: "I am not, however, very solicitious about the form, provided the business is but well completed."[9]

The House accepted Sherman's proposition and voted to place the amendments at the end of the Constitution—which is where they reside today—rather than incorporate them into the text separately.

It was Roger Sherman who proposed placing the Bill of Rights amendments at the end of the Constitution, where they reside today.

Other Proposed Amendments

Some Anti-Federalists, such as Elbridge Gerry and Thomas Tudor Tucker, still tried to convince Congress to adopt more amendments to the Constitution. These amendments would have drastically reduced the power of Congress. Gerry remained an avowed Anti-Federalist concerned over the power of the new federal government.

On August 18, 1789, Tucker introduced seventeen amendments which would reduce Congress's taxing powers and ability to oversee congressional elections.[10]

In speaking about Congress's power to control congressional elections, Gerry said "farewell to the rights of the people, even to elect their own representatives."[11] The House rejected Tucker's proposed amendments. On August 22, Tucker introduced several other amendments. He again attacked the power of the federal government to levy taxes.[12]

Tucker chastised his colleagues, saying: "I do not see the arguments in favour of giving Congress this power in so strong a light as some gentlemen do: It will be to erect an imperium in imperio." (Latin for "a state within a state.").[13] Tucker feared Congress would become too strong under the Constitution.

Representative James Jackson from Georgia, who earlier had opposed taking up the Bill of Rights issue, came to Madison's defense on the taxation issue: "Without the power of raising money to defray the expenses of government, how are we to secure against foreign invasion?"[14]

This process was not easy. James Madison even wrote to a friend that the process of amending the Constitution and amending the Bill of Rights had become a "nauseous project."[15]

However, on August 24, the House approved seventeen amendments "by way of appendix" to the Constitution. This means that the amendments would be added to the end of the Constitution.

The Senate passed its version of the amendments on September 9. This version included twelve amendments. The Senate operated behind closed doors until February 1794. Therefore, historians do not have as much information about the Senate debates as the House debates.

However, one of the most important actions the Senate took was the deletion of Madison's original amendment number five: "No state shall violate the equal rights of conscience, or the freedom of the press, or the trial by jury in criminal cases." Madison considered this the most important amendment.

With great foresight, Madison predicted that state governments would violate individual liberty as much as the federal government. Unfortunately, the Senate removed this amendment.

The removal of this proposal by the Senate would have a major impact on constitutional law. It would take the passage of the Fourteenth Amendment and twentieth century United States Supreme Court opinions to extend the protections of the Bill of Rights to the states.

Both houses of Congress agreed to the Senate version on September 25. The amendments now had to be ratified by the states.

Ratification of the Bill of Rights

On October 2, 1789, President George Washington, the beloved hero of the Revolutionary War whom nearly all politicians wanted to be America's first leader, officially sent the proposed amendments to the states for ratification. In order to take effect, three fourths of the state legislatures would have to approve of the amendments.

Media coverage of governmental bodies in the 1790s was nothing like what we have today. Therefore, historians know little about what occurred in the various legislatures. Legal historian Bernard Schwartz writes that "even the contemporary newspapers are virtually silent on the ratification debates in the states.[16]

The necessary number of states ratified ten of the twelve amendments. The first two original amendments dealt with the number of congressional representatives and congressional pay raises. They were not ratified by enough states. Thus, they were dropped from the Bill of Rights.

The ten ratified amendments that became known as the Bill of Rights took effect on December 15, 1791, when Virginia ratified them. This date is considered the birth of the Bill of Rights. Little attention was paid to the official ratification of the Bill of Rights.

Historian Robert Goldwin says that ratification became something of an "anticlimax" because the general public had already "been won over to the Constitution."[17] He argues that the public overcame its concern once both houses of Congress had approved the amendments. He concludes: "By the time they were ratified, the amendments were the solution to a problem that had ceased to exist."[18]

However, there was a problem with the Bill of Rights. It did not extend protection for individual liberty from state governments.

The Bill of Rights and State Governments

The Bill of Rights provided written guarantees of individual liberty. These guarantees assured that the federal government would not infringe on certain rights, such as the right to practice one's religion freely.

However, remember that the First Congress failed to approve James Madison's original amendment number five, the one that he had called the "most valuable." Madison's proposed amendment would have ensured that the different state governments could not infringe on certain individual liberties, such as "the right of conscience, freedom of the press, or trial by jury in criminal cases."

Madison proposed this amendment because he thought there needed to be a "double security." He believed state officials were "as liable to attack these invaluable privileges" as the federal government.[19] Only one member of the House spoke against the measure. Representative Tucker said it was more prudent "to leave the State Governments to themselves."[20] Madison's measure was dropped in the Senate.

This meant that the protections in the Bill of Rights did not apply to state governments. The United States Supreme Court made this clear in its 1833 decision *Barron v. Baltimore.*[21]

John Barron alleged that the city of Baltimore violated his constitutional rights by ruining his wharf. The city had engaged in construction activities that had damaged Barron's property. Barron wanted the city to pay for the damage to his dock. Barron said that the city had taken away his property without just compensation in violation of the fifth amendment. The city officials countered that they were acting for the general welfare of the city by improving the city streets.

The Supreme Court and Marshall reasoned that if the First Congress and the Founding Fathers had intended for the Bill of Rights to apply to the states, then "they

Chief Justice John Marshall led a strongly Federalist Supreme Court. In the 1833 Barron v. Baltimore *ruling, the Court said the Bill of Rights did not apply to state or local officials—only the federal government.*

would have declared this purpose in plain and intelligible language."[22] Madison had intended the Bill of Rights to apply to the state governments with one of his proposed amendments.

The theory behind applying the Bill of Rights only to the federal government was that the federal government was the greatest threat to individual liberty. Citizens' control over state governments seemed to some to serve as an adequate shield against state and local governments.

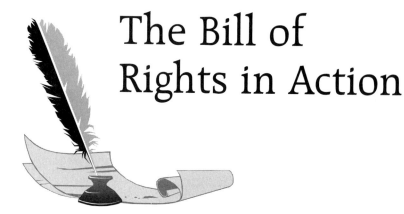

The Bill of Rights in Action

The protections of the Bill of Rights safeguard citizens from invasions of their constitutional rights by government officials—federal, state, or local. The protections of the Bill of Rights also extend to public school students.

The Right of Free Speech in Public Schools

In 1965, several public school students in Iowa decided to wear black armbands to school to protest U.S. involvement in the Vietnam War. When school officials learned of the plan, they quickly passed a no-armband rule. They feared that the armbands would create a disruption at the school.

Even though they faced a suspension, Christopher Eckhardt, John Tinker, and Mary Beth Tinker wore the armbands to school. School authorities suspended the students. They responded with a federal lawsuit that went all the way up to the United States Supreme Court.

In its 1969 decision *Tinker* v. *Des Moines Independent Community School District*, the High Court ruled 7-2 in favor of the students.[1] The Court determined that the students' act of wearing the black armbands was a form of symbolic speech entitled to First Amendment protection.

The High Court wrote that schools are not places of tyranny, but places where young people learn the lessons of democracy. The Court set up a standard that was highly protective of student expression.

Under the *Tinker* standard, school officials cannot censor student expression unless they can reasonably show that the expression would cause a substantial disruption at school.

In the 1980s, a more conservative Supreme Court cut back on the protections for student expression. High school student Matthew Fraser gave a nominating speech before his student body in which he used sexual references. School officials suspended him, saying his speech was too vulgar. Fraser challenged his suspension in court.

In 1986, the United States Supreme Court ruled in favor of the school officials in *Bethel School District No. 403 v. Fraser.*[2] The Court distinguished Fraser's lewd speech from the political speech of the students in the *Tinker* case. In its opinion, the Supreme Court also wrote that "the constitutional rights of students in public school are not automatically coextensive with the rights of adults in other settings."[3]

Two years later the United States Supreme Court again ruled against high school students in *Hazelwood School District v. Kuhlmeier.*[4] A group of students sued after an assistant school principal ordered the removal of two stories from a school newspaper. The stories concerned teen pregnancy and the impact of divorce on kids. The Supreme Court reasoned that school officials have greater leeway to control school-sponsored expression, such as a school newspaper, than student-initiated speech, such as the wearing of armbands.

Many public schools now are embroiled in controversies over school uniforms, dress codes, rock band T-shirts, and Confederate flag garb. Several students have also been suspended for critical comments they have written on their own Web sites.

Burning the Flag as a Form of Political Protest

The United States Supreme Court has determined that burning the flag as a political protest is a form of free speech.

In 1984, Gregory "Joey" Johnson burned an American flag outside the Republican National Convention in Dallas, Texas. Johnson said he engaged in this act in order to protest policies of the Reagan administration and certain Dallas-based corporations.

Johnson burned the flag in front of the Dallas City Hall while other protesters chanted: "America, the red, white, and blue, we spit on you."[5] Texas officials charged Johnson with violating a state law prohibiting desecration of venerated objects.

The statute defined desecrate as damaging or mistreating a venerated object, such as the American flag, knowing that it will seriously offend someone.

Texas officials charged Johnson under a state law prohibiting the desecration of the American flag. Johnson contended that this violated his First Amendment right to express himself on political matters.

The Supreme Court ruled 5-4 in *Texas* v. *Johnson* that the state could not convict Johnson and remain consistent with the First Amendment.[6] The majority noted that Johnson's act of burning the flag was a form of "expressive conduct" similar to pure speech.

Justice William Brennan said that state officials cannot create a "separate judicial category" for the flag. The majority said that our Founding Fathers "were not known

Justice William Brennan (front row, at far right) was part of the Warren Court, which often ruled in favor of expanded rights for individuals and the federal government.

for their reverence of the Union Jack."[7] In other words, some Founding Fathers had burned the British flag as a form of political protest during the Revolutionary War era. Justice Brennan wrote: "If there is a bedrock [fundamental] principle underlying the First Amendment, it is that the government may not prohibit the expression of an idea, simply because society finds the idea itself offensive or disagreeable."[8]

After this decision, Congress passed a law called the Flag Protection Act. This law made it a federal crime to desecrate the American flag.

In 1990, the Supreme Court ruled 5-4 in *United States* v. *Eichmann* that the federal law violated the Constitution.[9] "Punishing desecration of the flag dilutes the very freedom that makes this emblem so revered, and worth revering," wrote Justice Brennan.[10]

In recent years, Congress has considered several proposals to amend the Constitution to prohibit flag burning. Several times, the measure has passed the House of Representatives but has fallen a few votes short in the Senate.

Free Speech on the Internet

The First Amendment applies to different modes of communication, including newspapers, radio, television, and the Internet.

In 1996, Congress passed a federal law known as the Communications Decency Act. Parts of that law were designed to protect children from "patently offensive" and "indecent" online speech.

The American Civil Liberties Union (ACLU) and numerous other groups challenged the law, contending that the ban on indecent speech would infringe on the rights of adults and older minors.

The government argued that the law was necessary to protect minors from harmful material on the Internet.

In 1997, the United States Supreme Court sided with the ACLU. It ruled in *Reno* v. *ACLU* that speech on the Internet deserves the highest degree of First Amendment protection. The Court recognized that in many ways the Internet is the ultimate First Amendment fantasy. It empowers the average citizen to become both publisher and pamphleteer.

Legislators continue to pass laws to regulate pornography on the Internet. They justify these laws based on the protection of minors. Opponents of these laws contend that the laws fail to distinguish between older and younger minors. For instance, some free-speech advocates say that older minors should have access to online information about birth control, date rape, and other issues that may affect their daily lives.

After the demise of sections of the Communications Decency Act, Congress passed a new law regulating speech on the Internet, called the Child Online Protection Act. Some lower federal courts have ruled this law violates the First Amendment. The Supreme Court is expected to rule on the law in 2002.

In 2000, Congress passed a law called the Internet Children's Protection Act. This law requires public schools and libraries to filter the Internet to receive federal funds for Internet hook-ups. The ACLU has also challenged this law on First Amendment grounds.

Prayer in Public Schools

Prayer was commonplace in America's public schools in the twentieth century. The United States changed this landscape of school-sponsored prayer in schools in the 1960s.

In 1962, the United States Supreme Court determined in *Engel* v. *Vitale* that school-sponsored prayer violated the establishment clause of the First Amendment.[11] This was one of the most controversial decisions in the history of the United States Supreme Court. It remains a controversial issue.

The *Vitale* case concerned a procedure adopted by the New York Board of Regents to require students to say a prayer out loud in their classrooms at the beginning of each school day.

The state officials believed that the prayer would help school officials instill morality and spiritual training in their students.

However, the parents of ten students sued in federal court. They contended that the forced prayer violated the establishment clause and the principle of separation between church and state.

The United States Supreme Court ruled 6-1 that the practice violated the establishment clause.[12] The majority wrote that the government has no business composing "official prayers for any group of the American people"— even students. The Court's majority opinion did not cite a single case in its opinion. Instead, it spoke about the history of religious persecution suffered by our early colonists, stating that "this very practice of establishing governmentally composed prayers for religious services was one of the reasons which caused many of our early colonists to leave England and seek religious freedom in America."[13]

Justice Potter Stewart dissented, writing that the Court had "misapplied a great constitutional principle." Stewart pointed out that in 1954, Congress had added the phrase "one Nation under God, indivisible, with liberty and justice for all" to the Pledge of Allegiance. He noted that since 1865 American coins have contained the message "In God We Trust."[14]

However, the Supreme Court in many of its school prayer rulings has pointed out that children are impressionable and could feel coerced into joining in prayers that might be contrary to their faith.

The debate over school prayer continues to divide Americans and even Supreme Court justices. In 2000, the United States Supreme Court ruled 6-3 in *Santa Fe Independent School District* v. *Doe* that the practice of allowing students to pray over the loudspeaker at high school football games violated the establishment clause.[15]

The Court was concerned about those students at the game who did not subscribe to the religious beliefs of the majority. The Court determined that the policy "does nothing to protect minority views but rather places the students who hold such views at the mercy of the majority."[16]

The court reasoned that the audience would perceive the pregame prayer as an expression endorsed by the school administration. Chief Justice William Rehnquist dissented, or disagreed. He wrote that the Court's opinion "bristles with hostility to all things religious in public life."[17]

Other contentious issues involving the establishment clause in public schools include the teaching of creationism and school vouchers. The Supreme Court has struck down state laws that prohibited the teaching of evolution instead of creationism. The High Court has not yet ruled on a school voucher program. Under these programs, parents receive monies to send their children to other schools, including religious schools.

Americans are deeply divided over the meaning of the establishment clause. This division will not likely disappear in the near future.

Second Amendment

Many have argued that the Second Amendment guarantees the right to bear arms. Others argue that the Second Amendment guarantees only a collective right to bear arms. They contend that the right to bear arms is guaranteed only to the state's need to maintain a militia.

The United States Supreme Court has decided only a couple of Second Amendment cases. In 1939, the Court ruled that the National Firearms Act of 1934, which required registration of certain firearms, did not violate the Second Amendment.

In 1980, the Court rejected a Second Amendment challenge to federal laws regulating the use of firearms by persons who had been convicted of felonies.

Lower federal courts have upheld various other federal laws regulating the use of certain firearms, such as machine guns.

Controversy over the Second Amendment has not subsided. Several communities have attempted to regulate the possession of handguns. In the early 1980s, the village of Morton Grove, Illinois, became the first city in the United States to ban handguns.

Victor Quilici, an attorney, challenged the law in court. He argued that the city law violated the Second Amendment. However, a federal appeals court concluded that the Second Amendment did not extend to state and local governments. The appeals court also determined that the right to bear arms dealt with militias, not individuals.

Third Amendment

The Third Amendment was passed by the Founding Fathers to ensure that the American government never quartered, or housed, troops in its citizens' homes against their will.

The amendment has little relevance today. However, in 1982, a federal appeals court interpreted the meaning of the Third Amendment. The case arose after a statewide strike of prison guards in the state of New York.

During the strike, the Mid-Orange Correctional Facility in Warwick, New York, evicted several striking prison guards from their homes at the prison facility. The state housed members of the National Guard in the guards' facility-residences.

Two guards at Mid-Orange sued on Third Amendment grounds. They argued the housing of the National Guard was akin to the British housing troops in the colonists' homes.

A federal appeals court determined that the National Guardsmen were "soldiers" within the meaning of the

Third Amendment. The appeals court also ruled that the Third Amendment protected the guards even though they did not own homes, but lived in rooms at the prison complex.

The appeals court also determined that the guards had a "legitimate expectation of privacy protected by the Third Amendment."[18] Even though the guards eventually lost their suit on other grounds, the case was important because a federal court had finally interpreted the meaning of the Third Amendment.

Fourth Amendment

The Fourth Amendment protects people from unreasonable search and seizure by government officials. In its 1967 decision *Katz* v. *United States,* the United States Supreme Court had to determine the scope of the Fourth Amendment.[19]

Charles Katz was convicted of interstate gambling based on wiretaps placed on a public telephone booth.

Law enforcement officials had bugged the public telephone without obtaining a warrant. The Fourth Amendment provides that the police must have probable cause to obtain a warrant to search a person.

In the *Katz* case, the government argued that the Court should create an exception to the general rule requiring a warrant for conversations over a public telephone. The majority of the Supreme Court disagreed, writing: "Wherever a man may be, he is entitled to know that he will remain free from unreasonable searches and seizures."[20]

Justice John Harlan agreed with the majority, but wrote a separate opinion, called a concurring opinion, that set the standard for search and seizure cases. According to Harlan, the question was whether a person has a "reasonable expectation of privacy."[21] A person must show an actual, subjective expectation of privacy and society must recognize this expectation as reasonable.

In other words, the person must indicate they believed they had a right to privacy. This is the subjective component. Then, society must believe this expectation reasonable. This is the objective part of the test.

Fourth Amendment cases still cause controversy. Locker searches, drug testing, electronic surveillance, Internet communications, and sobriety checkpoints on the highway are just a few of the current hot-button issues.

Harlan's "reasonable expectation of privacy" test is the one that the Court applies to numerous Fourth Amendment cases.

Americans have the most protection from unreasonable searches and seizures in their own homes.

In 1961, the Supreme Court extended Fourth Amendment protection to apartment renters even though they do not own their residences. Nearly thirty years later, the Supreme Court determined that overnight guests enjoy the same expectations of privacy as homeowners.

In 2000, the Court issued several Fourth Amendment rulings. For example, in *Florida* v. *J.L.*, the High Court threw out gun possession charges against a juvenile because of an unlawful search. In the case, an anonymous person called the police telling them that a young African-American male in a plaid shirt standing at a particular bus stop was carrying a gun.

The police went to the bus stop and spotted a black male in a plaid shirt. The individual was carrying a gun. However, the Supreme Court ruled unanimously that the police did not have enough reasonable suspicion to stop and frisk the defendant. The Court wrote that the police only had the "bare report of an unknown, unaccountable informant."[22]

In 2001, the Court determined that Indianapolis police

officers violated the Fourth Amendment by randomly stopping people to determine if they were carrying illegal drugs. The Court noted that the basis of the Fourth Amendment was "individualized suspicion."

Law enforcement officials are now under attack in some circles for use of "racial profiling"—stopping citizens based on skin color rather than individualized suspicion.

Fifth Amendment

On March 23, 1963, police arrested a young Latino named Ernesto Miranda on charges of kidnapping and raping a teenager in Phoenix, Arizona. Though the victim could not identify him, Miranda signed a confession after two hours of intense police questioning.

Three years later in 1966, the Supreme Court reversed his conviction in a controversial 5-4 decision. The Court determined that the confession could not be introduced into evidence because Miranda had not been warned that he had a right not to incriminate himself.

The Court ruled in *Miranda* v. *Arizona* that law enforcement officers violated a criminal defendant's Fifth Amendment rights by failing to tell him of his right to remain silent and right to have an attorney present during interrogation.

The majority noted that "custodial interrogation exacts a heavy toll on individual liberty and trades on the weakness of individuals."[23]

The High Court established certain safeguards to ensure that police don't force people to confess to crimes they possibly did not commit.

The majority established the following rule: "At the outset, if a person in custody is to be subjected to interrogation, he must first be informed in clear and unequivocal terms that he has the right to remain silent." This warning of the right to remain silent must be accompanied with the statement that "anything said can and will be used against the individual in court."[24]

The *Miranda* decision created great controversy. Critics argued that a guilty person should not be allowed to go free because of police mistakes.

Two years after the *Miranda* decision, Congress passed a federal law which applies a balancing test to determine whether statements made during interrogations can be admissible in court. Under this law, the absence of warnings does not automatically invalidate a confession.

In 2000, the Supreme Court struck down this federal law, ruling that Congress had attempted, by passing this law, to overrule the *Miranda* decision. The Supreme Court ruled 7-2 against overturning *Miranda*. According to the Court, it "has become embedded in routine police practice to the point where the warnings have become part of our national culture."[25]

Due Process

The Fifth Amendment contains one of the most important protections in the Constitution: due process. The amendment provides that we cannot "be deprived of life, liberty, or property without due process of law." Many constitutional cases decided by the Supreme Court deal with whether a person's due process rights have been violated.

Normally, people cannot lose their property or lose property interests without the government following proper procedure. If a person is not given notice and a hearing, then we say their procedural due process rights have been violated.

In 1975, the Supreme Court ruled in *Goss* v. *Lopez* that public school students could not be suspended without notice of the charges and a chance to present their side of the story. The High Court determined that public school students possess a property interest in their education.

Many due process claims are brought by people convicted of crimes. In 2000, the Supreme Court struck down a New Jersey hate crime law that allowed a judge, rather than a jury, to enhance a defendant's sentence if he was convicted.

Sixth Amendment

The Sixth Amendment guarantees criminal defendants a fair trial. In *Sheppard* v. *Maxwell,* the U.S. Supreme Court ruled that excessive pretrial publicity could compromise a defendant's fair-trial rights.

The Court noted that the behavior of the media at the trial unfairly influenced the jury and created "bedlam" in the courtroom. The Court determined that judges have several options to ensure a fair trial. These include changing the location, or venue, of the trial, and sequestering, or isolating, jurors from the community.

The constitutional rights of a defendant to a fair trial can sometimes clash with the First Amendment rights of a free press. The debate over cameras in the courtroom highlights the tension between these two rights.

Some attorneys and judges believe that cameras distort the judicial process, particularly in criminal cases. They argue that cameras cause attorneys to showboat. Others believe that cameras serve an important function of informing the public about the criminal justice system. They argue that trials, such as the O.J. Simpson criminal case and other cases televised on Court TV, allow more people to learn about our judicial system.

The Right to a Speedy Trial

The Sixth Amendment also provides a defendant with a right to a speedy trial. This clause prevents officials from keeping a defendant imprisoned for a lengthy period of time before a trial. If there were no provision for a speedy trial, an accused's defense could suffer. People's memories could fade and so-called exculpatory evidence (evidence showing defendant's innocence) could be lost.

In 1992, the United States Supreme Court ruled in *Doggett* v. *United States* that an accused's Sixth Amendment right to a speedy trial was violated by an eight-and-a-half year gap between his indictment and arrest.[26] The Court determined that the defendant would be prejudiced in trying to defend himself against charges filed years ago.

The Right to Confront One's Accusers

The confrontation clause of the Sixth Amendment provides: "In all criminal prosecutions, the accused shall enjoy the right . . . to be confronted with the witnesses against him."

The Supreme Court has recognized that face-to-face confrontation ensures greater reliability by reducing the risk that an innocent person will be convicted. The confrontation clause ensures that a witness must face cross-examination—a process by which a witness must answer questions by an attorney from the other side. The Court has referred to cross-examination as the "greatest legal engine ever invented for the discovery of truth."[27]

However, the Court has relaxed the requirements of the confrontation clause in child-abuse cases. In *Maryland* v. *Craig*, the U.S. Supreme Court ruled constitutional a Maryland law allowing child-abuse victims to testify by a one-way closed circuit television.

The Court reasoned that the state's interest in the physical and psychological well-being of children could outweigh a defendant's Sixth Amendment rights.

The Right to an Attorney

On August 4, 1961, a Florida man named Clarence Earl Gideon was tried and convicted of breaking and entering a pool hall. Before the trial, Gideon, who was too poor to afford a lawyer, had asked the court to appoint him counsel. Gideon said that "the United States Supreme Court says I am to be represented by counsel."[28]

The Sixth Amendment of the Constitution seemed to support Gideon's position. It provides that in criminal prosecutions, the accused should "have the assistance of counsel for his defence."

However, the Sixth Amendment was held to apply only in federal courts. Gideon had been tried and convicted in a Florida state court. Gideon had argued in vain that the protections of the Sixth Amendment should also apply in state courts via the Fourteenth Amendment.

The United States Supreme Court had ruled in its 1942 decision *Betts* v. *Brady* that the appointment of counsel was not a fundamental right for those tried in state court. Gideon had to argue that the Betts case should be overturned.

In its 1963 decision *Gideon* v. *Wainwright,* the U.S. Supreme Court overruled the holding of Betts. The Court wrote that "the right of one charged with crime to counsel may not be deemed fundamental and essential to fair trials in some countries, but it is in ours."[29]

The Court concluded that "this noble ideal cannot be realized if the poor man charged with crime has to face his accusers without a lawyer to assist him."

Seventh Amendment

The Seventh Amendment guarantees a right to a jury trial in civil cases. This amendment has not been extended to the states. Thus, the right to a jury trial is guaranteed by the Bill of Rights only for the federal civil cases.

The last clause of the Seventh Amendment provides that "no fact tried by a jury shall be otherwise re-examined in any Court of the United States, than according to the rules of the common law." This provision ensures that a jury's decision on the facts must stand unless it is clearly in error. In our country, juries determine questions of fact, while judges determine questions of law.

Excessive Bail

The first clause of the Eighth Amendment provides protection from "excessive bail." Bail is defined as security given to release an accused person pending trial.

Too often in our history, persons accused of crimes remained in jail until their trial because they could not afford to pay enough money—or bail—to be released. In its 1951 decision *Stack* v. *Boyle,* the United States Supreme Court noted that people charged with non-capital crimes should be allowed bail. "Unless this right to bail is preserved, the presumption of innocence, secured only after centuries of struggle, would lose its meaning."[30]

In the *Boyle* case, twelve individuals accused of violating a federal law had bail set at $50,000 each. However, the trial judge had set bail at a much higher rate than normal for such offenses. The judge had acted without conducting a hearing to determine the likelihood of the defendants fleeing to avoid prosecution—one downfall of the legal system.

To set bail at a high amount without a hearing "would inject into our own system of government . . . totalitarianism," the Supreme Court wrote.[31]

Excessive Fines

The second clause of the Eighth Amendment prohibits "excessive fines." In 1998, the United States Supreme Court ruled that federal law enforcement officials violated this clause when they said that a defendant had to forfeit over $300,000 for refusing to report that he was carrying more than $10,000 in currency overseas.

Federal law provided that people had to report that they were carrying over $10,000 in currency. A related law said that failure to report could lead to forfeiture of the property.

Hosep Bajakajian failed to disclose that he was carrying well over $10,000 in cash. Because he violated a federal law, the government argued that he had to forfeit all the monies he was carrying, which turned out to be $357,144.

In a 5 to 4 decision, the United States Supreme Court determined that the "amount of the forfeiture was grossly disproportionate to the gravity of the defendant's offense."[32] The Court determined that the defendant's only crime was a reporting offense. The majority also reasoned that if the crime had not been detected, the only harm to the government was that it would not have known that "$357,144 had left the country."[33]

Cruel and Unusual Punishment

By far the most contentious Eighth Amendment issue is whether the death penalty constitutes "cruel and unusual punishment." In several states, such as Texas, many inmates are executed each year.

Social scientists and others debate whether the Eighth Amendment deters violent crime. Others question whether the death penalty is administered fairly. In 1986, the United States Supreme Court confronted a case in which there was statistical evidence that the killers of white victims were far more likely to receive the death penalty than those who murdered black victims.[34] Warren McClesky, a black man convicted in 1978 of killing a white police officer in Georgia, argued that the state's capital punishment system was unconstitutional because of racial bias.

The United States Supreme Court rejected McClesky's claim by a 5-4 vote. The majority recognized that the statistical evidence appeared to show sentencing discrepancies based on race. The majority reasoned, however, that McClesky could not show that improper racial factors affected his particular case.

The majority of the Court also wrote that "apparent discrepancies in sentencing are an inevitable part of our criminal justice system."[35] In effect, the majority said that no punishment system was perfect.

Justice William Brennan and three other justices dissented. Brennan wrote that racial considerations of the victim should not play a role in a death-penalty decision.

The death penalty remains a tough and troubling issue. In 1994, Justice Harry Blackmun, who formerly supported the death penalty in cases in the 1970s, had a change of heart on the death penalty. He expressed this change in a passionate dissent in a 1994 death-penalty case.[36] "From this day forward, I no longer shall tinker with the machinery of death," Blackmun wrote.[37] He said that the death-penalty system was too fraught with "factual, legal and moral error."[38]

However, the majority of the United States Supreme Court still believes that the death penalty, fairly administered, does not violate the Eighth Amendment for those convicted of murder. However, the Court has ruled it an Eighth Amendment violation to sentence someone to death for other crimes. In *Coker* v. *Georgia,* the Supreme Court ruled that it violated the Eighth Amendment to sentence a person to death for the crime of rape.

The Court has also considered the Eighth Amendment's prohibition on cruel and unusual punishment outside of the death penalty context. For example, in a 1992 decision the U.S. Supreme Court ruled that prison officials violated the Eighth Amendment if they used excessive force against prisoners in a malicious manner. This principle also applies to the police.

The Court has also considered the issue in public schools. In *Ingrahamm* v. *Wright,* the Court ruled 5-4 that paddling does not raise an Eighth Amendment issue.[39]

The Ninth Amendment

The Constitution and the Bill of Rights does not explicitly provide a right of privacy. However, the United States Supreme Court beginning in the 1960s has determined that the Ninth Amendment creates privacy rights.

Remember that the Ninth Amendment says that the people possess more rights than those specifically enumerated, or listed, in the Constitution and the Bill of Rights. Congress included the Ninth Amendment to ensure that the people retained other rights not specifically listed in the other provisions of the Bill of Rights.

For more than a century, the Ninth Amendment remained a constitutional question mark. It was not even mentioned by the United States Supreme Court.

This changed in the 1965 decision *Griswold* v. *Connecticut* in which three Justices determined that the Ninth Amendment protected a general right of privacy for married people.[40]

Justice Arthur Goldberg, joined by Chief Justice Earl Warren and Justice William Brennan, wrote that "the right of privacy in the marital relation is fundamental and basic—a personal right that is 'retained by the people' within the meaning of the Ninth Amendment."[41]

Justice Harry Blackmun extended the Ninth Amendment's right to privacy to cover "a woman's decision whether or not to terminate her pregnancy" in the controversial *Roe* v. *Wade* decision in 1973.[42]

The Tenth Amendment

The Tenth Amendment is the only part of the Bill of Rights that does not refer to individual rights. This amendment limits the power of the federal government with respect to state governments.

The Tenth Amendment signifies the principle of federalism—the distribution of power between a central authority and its supporting units. Many members of the Supreme Court—such as Chief Justice William Rehnquist, and Justices Antonin Scalia and Clarence Thomas—are considered protectors of state rights.

In the 1995 decision *United States* v. *Lopez*, the majority struck down a 1990 federal law that created gun-free school zones. The justices determined that Congress did not have constitutional authority to regulate in this issue of state and local concern.

The majority of the Supreme Court determined that Congress had not demonstrated a strong enough connection with interstate commerce to pass the law under the commerce clause. They believed the state or local government should pass such a law.

In 1997, the Supreme Court again struck down a federal law in part on Tenth Amendment grounds. In *Printz* v. *United States*, the Court examined the so-called

Under Chief Justice William Rehnquist, the Supreme Court has often appeared more conservative than in years past, but it has still upheld wide provisions for individual rights.

Brady Act, which required local law enforcement officials to conduct background checks on people wanting to buy handguns.

The Court ruled 5-4 that the federal government could not force states to run a federal program. According to the majority, the "mandatory obligation" to run background checks "plainly runs afoul of that rule."[43]

Conclusion

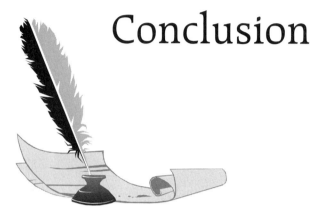

The Bill of Rights gives us "the great rights of mankind."[1] It ensures that we have to right to criticize the government and practice our own religious faiths. It ensures that the government must afford us due process of law before taking away our liberty or property. It guarantees that law enforcement officials cannot invade our privacy without very good reason.

Extending the Promise of the Bill of Rights

We must also recognize that the promise of the Bill of Rights was delayed to many people in our society, particularly African Americans and women.

The Bill of Rights and the three amendments passed during Reconstruction (period after the Civil War)—the Thirteenth, Fourteenth and Fifteenth amendments—have provided a legal framework during which social progress has been able to evolve to fulfill the promise of liberty to all.

Originally, the Supreme Court ruled that the Bill of Rights did not apply to the states. This ruling would have a devastating impact on individual liberty. The protections of the Bill of Rights did not begin to apply to state and local governments until the adoption of the Fourteenth Amendment in 1868 and later United States Supreme Court decisions. That amendment provided in part:

> No State shall make or enforce any law which shall abridge the privileges or immunities of citizens of the United States; nor shall any State deprive any person of life, liberty, or property without due process of law; nor deny to any person within its jurisdiction the equal protection of the laws.

The primary author of the Fourteenth Amendment, Representative John Bingham of Ohio, had argued that the amendment made the Bill of Rights applicable to the states. However, it was many years before the United States Supreme Court took this position.

The United States Supreme Court began a process of selectively applying different parts of the Bill of Rights to the states through the Fourteenth Amendment. Beginning in the twentieth century, the Court "has used selective incorporation to make almost all the specific guarantees of the bill of rights applicable to the states."[2]

When the Constitution and the Bill of Rights were adopted, only privileged white males benefited. African Americans and women did not make substantial advancements until the twentieth century. Blacks were denied basic civil rights. Many of these rights did not come to fruition until the civil rights movement of the 1950s and 1960s. Women did not receive the right to vote until the twentieth century.

The freedoms of the Bill of Rights enabled women and minorities to advocate for social change. The First Amendment was essential to the women's suffrage movement of the 1910s and the civil rights movement of the 1950s and 1960s.

The freedoms protected under the Bill of Rights have allowed Americans to show their support—or disapproval— of the policies of the government. This often led to great changes, as occurred through the efforts of women suffragists, who marched and petitioned to win the right to vote.

Women suffragists assembled and marched in the streets to petition for social change. Using this example, African Americans engaged in peaceful forms of protest, such as sit-ins, to petition for progress.

Adapting to the Future and Protecting the Minority

The Founding Fathers created a legal system that has been able to adapt and create a more equal society. It has been called by many a "living Constitution." That means that the principles of the Constitution can adapt to changing times.

For example, the Founding Fathers could not have imagined the powers of the Internet. However, they created a First Amendment in a time of the print medium to protect this mode of communication.

The Bill of Rights should be especially valued by the nation's youth. More than fifty-five years ago, United States Supreme Court Justice Robert Jackson noted that school board officials must ensure that public school students learn the lessons of the Bill of Rights. Jackson wrote:

> That they are educating the young for citizenship is reason for scrupulous protection of Constitutional freedoms of the individual, if we are not to strangle the free mind at its source and teach youth to discount important principles of government as mere platitudes.[3]

Concerned citizens must take an active role to ensure that our government officials do not infringe on these precious liberties. Too often we take these rights for granted.

Polls show that many Americans do not support many of the freedoms in the Bills of Rights. Often, civil liberties are viewed as a shield for criminals or those with unpopular views.

However, we must remember that the Bill of Rights is in large part designed to protect the rights of those whose ideas conflict with the majority. Criminal defendants cite the protections of the Fourth, Fifth, and Sixth Amendments when they are charged with crimes. Unpopular speakers wrap themselves in the mantle of the First Amendment when conveying their views. Prisoners often bring claims of excessive punishment under the Eighth Amendment.

Just because we do not respect a particular person or his or her views, does not mean we should disrespect the Bill of Rights. Justice Felix Frankfurter once expressed it this way: "It is a fair summary of history to say that the safeguards of liberty have frequently been forged in controversies involving not very nice people."[4]

Protecting the rights of those with whom we disagree or those who are most powerless ensures that the rights of all Americans will be protected. And that is the real lesson of the Bill of Rights.

Author Nat Hentoff writes that "Unless more Americans know the Constitution and live the Bill of Rights, the future of the nation as a strongly functioning constitutional democracy will be at risk."[5]

As the future leaders of our nation, young people must understand and appreciate the fragility of our precious freedoms. The United States Supreme Court is constantly making decisions that impact on our fundamental freedoms in the Bill of Rights.

The Founding Fathers started a revolution to establish a country free from the shackles of the English monarch. They declared their independence. Hundreds of thousands of Americans have died on fields of battle to preserve our freedom.

But threats to freedom come not only from external enemies, but from well-intentioned people in our own country. Louis Brandeis, a great former justice of the United States Supreme Court once wrote: "The greatest dangers to liberty lurk in insidious encroachment by men of zeal, well-meaning but without understanding."[6]

These dangers to liberty are even greater for young people. Today's students live in a time when government leaders wish to regulate rock and rap music, video games, movies and the Internet to protect minors.[7] The efforts are often well-meaning, but they do affect fundamental freedoms.

The Bill of Rights are too precious and too important to be sacrificed for other goals. They are truly the "Great Rights of Mankind."

THE CONSTITUTION OF THE UNITED STATES

The text of the Constitution is presented here. All words are given their modern spelling and capitalization. Brackets [ ] indicate parts that have been changed or set aside by amendments.

Preamble

We the People of the United States, in Order to form a more perfect Union, establish Justice, insure domestic Tranquillity, provide for the common defence, promote the general Welfare, and secure the Blessings of Liberty to ourselves and our Posterity, do ordain and establish this Constitution for the United States of America.

ARTICLE I

The Legislative Branch

Section 1. All legislative powers herein granted shall be vested in a Congress of the United States, which shall consist of a Senate and House of Representatives.

The House of Representatives

Section 2. (1) The House of Representatives shall be composed of members chosen every second year by the people of the several states, and the electors in each state shall have the qualifications requisite for electors of the most numerous branch of the state legislature.

(2) No person shall be a Representative who shall not have attained to the age of twenty five years, and been seven years a citizen of the United States, and who shall not, when elected, be an inhabitant of that state in which he shall be chosen.

(3) Representatives and direct taxes shall be apportioned among the several states which may be included within this union, according to their respective numbers, [which shall be determined by adding to the whole number of free persons, including those bound to service for a term of years, and excluding Indians not taxed, three fifths of all other persons]. The actual Enumeration shall be made within three years after the first meeting of the Congress of the United States, and within every subsequent term of ten years, in such manner as they shall by law direct. The number of Representatives shall not exceed one for every thirty thousand, but each state shall have at least one Representative; [and until such enumeration shall be made, the state of New Hampshire shall be entitled to chuse three, Massachusetts eight, Rhode Island and Providence Plantations one, Connecticut five, New York six, New Jersey four, Pennsylvania eight, Delaware one, Maryland six, Virginia ten, North Carolina five, South Carolina five, and Georgia three].

(4) When vacancies happen in the Representation from any state, the executive authority thereof shall issue writs of election to fill such vacancies.

(5) The House of Representatives shall choose their speaker and other officers; and shall have the sole power of impeachment.

The Senate

Section 3. (1) The Senate of the United States shall be composed of two Senators from each state, [chosen by the legislature thereof,] for six years; and each Senator shall have one vote.

(2) Immediately after they shall be assembled in consequence of the first election, they shall be divided as equally as may be into three classes. The seats of the Senators of the first class shall be vacated at the expiration of the second year, of the second class at the expiration of the fourth year, and the third class at the expiration of the sixth year, so that one third may be chosen every second year; [and if vacancies happen by resignation, or otherwise, during the recess of the legislature of any state, the executive thereof may make temporary appointments until the next meeting of the legislature, which shall then fill such vacancies].

(3) No person shall be a Senator who shall not have attained to the age of thirty years, and been nine years a citizen of the United States and who shall not, when elected, be an inhabitant of that state for which he shall be chosen.

(4) The Vice President of the United States shall be President of the Senate, but shall have no vote, unless they be equally divided.

(5) The Senate shall choose their other officers, and also a President pro tempore, in the absence of the Vice President, or when he shall exercise the office of President of the United States.

(6) The Senate shall have the sole power to try all impeachments. When sitting for that purpose, they shall be on oath or affirmation. When the President of the United States is tried, the Chief Justice shall preside: And no person shall be convicted without the concurrence of two thirds of the members present.

(7) Judgment in cases of impeachment shall not extend further than to removal from office, and disqualification to hold and enjoy any office of honor, trust or profit under the United States: but the party convicted shall nevertheless be liable and subject to indictment, trial, judgment and punishment, according to law.

Organization of Congress

Section 4. (1) The times, places and manner of holding elections for Senators and Representatives, shall be prescribed in each state by the legislature thereof; but the Congress may at any time by law make or alter such regulations, [except as to the places of choosing Senators].

(2) The Congress shall assemble at least once in every year, [and such meeting shall be on the first Monday in December], unless they shall by law appoint a different day.

Section 5. (1) Each House shall be the judge of the elections, returns and qualifications of its own members, and a majority of each shall constitute a quorum to do business; but a smaller number may adjourn from day to day, and may be authorized to compel the attendance of absent members, in such manner, and under such penalties as each House may provide.

(2) Each House may determine the rules of its proceedings, punish its members for disorderly behavior, and, with the concurrence of two thirds, expel a member.

(3) Each House shall keep a journal of its proceedings, and from time to time publish the same, excepting such parts as may in their judgment require secrecy; and the yeas and nays of the members of either House on any question shall, at the desire of one fifth of those present, be entered on the journal.

(4) Neither House, during the session of Congress, shall, without the consent of the other, adjourn for more than three days, nor to any other place than that in which the two Houses shall be sitting.

Section 6. (1) The Senators and Representatives shall receive a compensation for their services, to be ascertained by law, and paid out of the treasury of the United States. They shall in all cases, except treason, felony and breach of the peace, be privileged from arrest during their attendance at the session of their respective Houses, and in going to and returning from the same; and for any speech or debate in either House, they shall not be questioned in any other place.

(2) No Senator or Representative shall, during the time for which he was elected, be appointed to any civil office under the authority of the United States, which shall have been created, or the emoluments whereof shall have been increased during such time: and no person holding any

office under the United States, shall be a member of either House during his continuance in office.

Section 7. (1) All bills for raising revenue shall originate in the House of Representatives; but the Senate may propose or concur with amendments as on other Bills.

(2) Every bill which shall have passed the House of Representatives and the Senate, shall, before it become a law, be presented to the President of the United States; if he approve he shall sign it, but if not he shall return it, with his objections to that House in which it shall have originated, who shall enter the objections at large on their journal, and proceed to reconsider it. If after such reconsideration two thirds of that House shall agree to pass the bill, it shall be sent, together with the objections, to the other House, by which it shall likewise be reconsidered, and if approved by two thirds of that House, it shall become a law. But in all such cases the votes of both Houses shall be determined by yeas and nays, and the names of the persons voting for and against the bill shall be entered on the journal of each House respectively. If any bill shall not be returned by the President within ten days (Sundays excepted) after it shall have been presented to him, the same shall be a law, in like manner as if he had signed it, unless the Congress by their adjournment prevent its return, in which case it shall not be a law.

(3) Every order, resolution, or vote to which the concurrence of the Senate and House of Representatives may be necessary (except on a question of adjournment) shall be presented to the President of the United States; and before the same shall take effect, shall be approved by him, or being disapproved by him, shall be repassed by two thirds of the Senate and House of Representatives, according to the rules and limitations prescribed in the case of a bill.

POWERS GRANTED TO CONGRESS
The Congress shall have the power:

Section 8. (1) To lay and collect taxes, duties, imposts and excises, to pay the debts and provide for the common defense and general welfare of the United States; but all duties, imposts and excises shall be uniform throughout the United States;

(2) To borrow money on the credit of the United States;

(3) To regulate commerce with foreign nations, and among the several states, and with the Indian tribes;

(4) To establish a uniform rule of naturalization, and uniform laws on the subject of bankruptcies throughout the United States;

(5) To coin money, regulate the value thereof, and of foreign coin, and fix the standard of weights and measures;

(6) To provide for the punishment of counterfeiting the securities and current coin of the United States;

(7) To establish post offices and post roads;

(8) To promote the progress of science and useful arts, by securing for limited times to authors and inventors the exclusive right to their respective writings and discoveries;

(9) To constitute tribunals inferior to the Supreme Court;

(10) To define and punish piracies and felonies committed on the high seas, and offenses against the law of nations;

(11) To declare war, grant letters of marque and reprisal, and make rules concerning captures on land and water;

(12) To raise and support armies, but no appropriation of money to that use shall be for a longer term than two years;

(13) To provide and maintain a navy;

(14) To make rules for the government and regulation of the land and naval forces;

(15) To provide for calling forth the militia to execute the laws of the union, suppress insurrections and repel invasions;

(16) To provide for organizing, arming, and disciplining, the militia, and for governing such part of them as may be employed in the service of the United States, reserving to the states respectively, the appointment of the officers, and the authority of training the militia according to the discipline prescribed by Congress;

(17) To exercise exclusive legislation in all cases whatsoever, over such District (not exceeding ten miles square) as may, by cession of particular states, and the acceptance of Congress, become the seat of the government of the United States, and to exercise like authority over all places purchased by the consent of the legislature of the state in which the same shall be, for the erection of forts, magazines, arsenals, dockyards, and other needful buildings;—And

(18) To make all laws which shall be necessary and proper for carrying into execution the foregoing powers, and all other powers vested by this Constitution in the government of the United States, or in any department or officer thereof.

Powers Forbidden to Congress

Section 9. (1) The migration or importation of such persons as any of the states now existing shall think proper to admit, shall not be prohibited by the Congress prior to the year one thousand eight hundred and eight, but a tax or duty may be imposed on such importation, not exceeding ten dollars for each person.

(2) The privilege of the writ of *habeas corpus* shall not be suspended, unless when in cases of rebellion or invasion the public safety may require it.

(3) No bill of attainder or *ex post facto* Law shall be passed.

(4) No capitation, [or other direct,] tax shall be laid, unless in proportion to the census or enumeration herein before directed to be taken.

(5) No tax or duty shall be laid on articles exported from any state.

(6) No preference shall be given by any regulation of commerce or revenue to the ports of one state over those of another: nor shall vessels bound to, or from, one state, be obliged to enter, clear or pay duties in another.

(7) No money shall be drawn from the treasury, but in consequence of appropriations made by law; and a regular statement and account of receipts and expenditures of all public money shall be published from time to time.

(8) No title of nobility shall be granted by the United States: and no person holding any office of profit or trust under them, shall, without the consent of the Congress, accept of any present, emolument, office, or title, of any kind whatever, from any king, prince, or foreign state.

Powers Forbidden to the States

Section 10. (1) No state shall enter into any treaty, alliance, or confederation; grant letters of marque and reprisal; coin money; emit bills of credit; make anything but gold and silver coin a tender in payment of debts; pass any bill of attainder, *ex post facto* law, or law impairing the obligation of contracts, or grant any title of nobility.

(2) No state shall, without the consent of the Congress, lay any imposts or duties on imports or exports, except what may be absolutely necessary for executing its inspection laws: and the net produce of all duties and imposts, laid by any state on imports or exports, shall be for the use of the treasury of the United States; and all such laws shall be subject to the revision and control of the Congress.

(3) No state shall, without the consent of Congress, lay any duty of tonnage, keep troops, or ships of war in time of peace, enter into any agreement or compact with another state, or with a foreign power, or engage in war, unless actually invaded, or in such imminent danger as will not admit of delay.

ARTICLE II
The Executive Branch

Section 1. (1) The executive power shall be vested in a President of the United States of America. He shall hold his office during the term of four years, and, together with the Vice President, chosen for the same term, be elected, as follows:

(2) Each state shall appoint, in such manner as the Legislature thereof may direct, a number of electors, equal to the whole number of Senators and Representatives to which the State may be entitled in the Congress: but no Senator or Representative, or person holding an office of trust or profit under the United States, shall be appointed an elector.

(3) [The electors shall meet in their respective states, and vote by ballot for two persons, of whom one at least shall not be an inhabitant of the same state with themselves. And they shall make a list of all the persons voted for, and of the number of votes for each; which list they shall sign and certify, and transmit sealed to the seat of the government of the United States, directed to the President of the Senate. The President of the Senate shall, in the presence of the Senate and House of Representatives, open all the certificates, and the votes shall then be counted. The person having the greatest number of votes shall be the President, if such number be a majority of the whole number of electors appointed; and if there be more than one who have such majority, and have an equal number of votes, then the House of Representatives shall immediately choose by ballot one of them for President; and if no person have a majority, then from the five highest on the list the said House shall in like manner choose the

President. But in choosing the President, the votes shall be taken by States, the representation from each state having one vote; A quorum for this purpose shall consist of a member or members from two thirds of the states, and a majority of all the states shall be necessary to a choice. In every case, after the choice of the President, the person having the greatest number of votes of the electors shall be the Vice President. But if there should remain two or more who have equal votes, the Senate shall choose from them by ballot the Vice President.]

(4) The Congress may determine the time of choosing the electors, and the day on which they shall give their votes; which day shall be the same throughout the United States.

(5) No person except a natural born citizen, or a citizen of the United States, at the time of the adoption of this Constitution, shall be eligible to the office of President; neither shall any person be eligible to that office who shall not have attained to the age of thirty five years, and been fourteen Years a resident within the United States.

(6) In case of the removal of the President from office, or of his death, resignation, or inability to discharge the powers and duties of the said office, the same shall devolve on the Vice President, and the Congress may by law provide for the case of removal, death, resignation or inability, both of the President and Vice President, declaring what officer shall then act as President, and such officer shall act accordingly, until the disability be removed, or a President shall be elected.

(7) The President shall, at stated times, receive for his services, a compensation, which shall neither be increased nor diminished during the period for which he shall have

been elected, and he shall not receive within that period any other emolument from the United States, or any of them.

(8) Before he enter on the execution of his office, he shall take the following oath or affirmation:—"I do solemnly swear (or affirm) that I will faithfully execute the office of President of the United States, and will to the best of my ability, preserve, protect and defend the Constitution of the United States."

Section 2. (1) The President shall be commander in chief of the Army and Navy of the United States, and of the militia of the several states, when called into the actual service of the United States; he may require the opinion, in writing, of the principal officer in each of the executive departments, upon any subject relating to the duties of their respective offices, and he shall have power to grant reprieves and pardons for offenses against the United States, except in cases of impeachment.

(2) He shall have power, by and with the advice and consent of the Senate, to make treaties, provided two thirds of the Senators present concur; and he shall nominate, and by and with the advice and consent of the Senate, shall appoint ambassadors, other public ministers and consuls, judges of the Supreme Court, and all other officers of the United States, whose appointments are not herein otherwise provided for, and which shall be established by law: but the Congress may by law vest the appointment of such inferior officers, as they think proper, in the President alone, in the courts of law, or in the heads of departments.

(3) The President shall have power to fill up all vacancies that may happen during the recess of the Senate, by granting commissions which shall expire at the end of their next session.

Section 3. He shall from time to time give to the Congress information of the state of the union, and recommend to their consideration such measures as he shall judge necessary and expedient; he may, on extraordinary occasions, convene both Houses, or either of them, and in case of disagreement between them, with respect to the time of adjournment, he may adjourn them to such time as he shall think proper; he shall receive ambassadors and other public ministers; he shall take care that the laws be faithfully executed, and shall commission all the officers of the United States.

Section 4. The President, Vice President and all civil officers of the United States, shall be removed from office on impeachment for, and conviction of, treason, bribery, or other high crimes and misdemeanors.

ARTICLE III
The Judicial Branch

Section 1. The judicial power of the United States, shall be vested in one Supreme Court, and in such inferior courts as the Congress may from time to time ordain and establish. The judges, both of the supreme and inferior courts, shall hold their offices during good behaviour, and shall, at stated times, receive for their services, a compensation, which shall not be diminished during their continuance in office.

Section 2. (1) The judicial power shall extend to all cases, in law and equity, arising under this Constitution, the laws of the United States, and treaties made, or which shall be made, under their authority;—to all cases affecting ambassadors, other public ministers and consuls;—to all cases of admiralty and maritime jurisdiction;—to controversies to which the United States shall be a party;—to controversies between two or more states;[—between a state and citizens of another state;]—between citizens of different states;—between citizens of the same state claiming lands under grants of different states, and between a state, or the citizens thereof, and foreign states, [citizens or subjects].

(2) In all cases affecting ambassadors, other public ministers and consuls, and those in which a state shall be party, the Supreme Court shall have original jurisdiction. In all the other cases before mentioned, the Supreme Court shall have appellate jurisdiction, both as to law and fact, with such exceptions, and under such regulations as the Congress shall make.

(3) The trial of all crimes, except in cases of impeachment, shall be by jury; and such trial shall be held in the state where the said crimes shall have been committed; but when not committed within any state, the trial shall be at such place or places as the Congress may by law have directed.

Section 3. (1) Treason against the United States, shall consist only in levying war against them, or in adhering to their enemies, giving them aid and comfort. No person shall be convicted of treason unless on the testimony of two witnesses to the same overt act, or on confession in open court.

(2) The Congress shall have power to declare the punishment of treason, but no attainder of treason shall work corruption of blood, or forfeiture except during the life of the person attainted.

ARTICLE IV

Relation of the States to Each Other

Section 1. Full faith and credit shall be given in each state to the public acts, records, and judicial proceedings of every other state. And the Congress may by general laws prescribe the manner in which such acts, records, and proceedings shall be proved, and the effect thereof.

Section 2. (1) The citizens of each state shall be entitled to all privileges and immunities of citizens in the several states.

(2) A person charged in any state with treason, felony, or other crime, who shall flee from justice, and be found in another state, shall on demand of the executive authority of the state from which he fled, be delivered up, to be removed to the state having jurisdiction of the crime.

(3) [No person held to service or labor in one state, under the laws thereof, escaping into another, shall, in consequence of any law or regulation therein, be discharged from such service or labor, but shall be delivered up on claim of the party to whom such service or labor may be due.]

Federal-State Relations

Section 3. (1) New states may be admitted by the Congress into this union; but no new states shall be formed or erected within the jurisdiction of any other state; nor any state be formed by the junction of two or more states, or parts of states, without the consent of the legislatures of the states concerned as well as of the Congress.

(2) The Congress shall have power to dispose of and make all needful rules and regulations respecting the territory or other property belonging to the United States; and nothing in this Constitution shall be so construed as to prejudice any claims of the United States, or of any particular state.

Section 4. The United States shall guarantee to every state in this union a republican form of government, and shall protect each of them against invasion; and on application of the legislature, or of the executive (when the legislature cannot be convened) against domestic violence.

ARTICLE V
Amending the Constitution

The Congress, whenever two thirds of both houses shall deem it necessary, shall propose amendments to this Constitution, or, on the application of the legislatures of two thirds of the several states, shall call a convention for proposing amendments, which, in either case, shall be valid to all intents and purposes, as part of this Constitution, when ratified by the legislatures of three fourths of the several states, or by conventions in three fourths thereof, as the one or the other mode of ratification may be proposed by the Congress; provided [that no amendment which may be made prior to the year one thousand eight hundred and eight shall in any manner affect the first and fourth clauses in the ninth section of the first article; and] that no state, without its consent, shall be deprived of its equal suffrage in the Senate.

ARTICLE VI

National Debts

(1) All debts contracted and engagements entered into, before the adoption of this Constitution, shall be as valid against the United States under this Constitution, as under the Confederation.

Supremacy of the National Government

(2) This Constitution, and the laws of the United States which shall be made in pursuance thereof; and all treaties made, or which shall be made, under the authority of the United States, shall be the supreme law of the land; and the judges in every state shall be bound thereby, anything in the Constitution or laws of any State to the contrary notwithstanding.

(3) The Senators and Representatives before mentioned, and the members of the several state legislatures, and all executive and judicial officers, both of the United States and of the several states, shall be bound by oath or affirmation, to support this Constitution; but no religious test shall ever be required as a qualification to any office or public trust under the United States.

ARTICLE VII

Ratifying the Constitution

The ratification of the conventions of nine states, shall be sufficient for the establishment of this Constitution between the states so ratifying the same.

Done in convention by the unanimous consent of the states present the seventeenth day of September in the year of our Lord one thousand seven hundred and eighty seven and of the independence of the United States of America the twelfth. In witness whereof We have hereunto subscribed our Names.

Amendments to the Constitution

The first ten amendments, known as the Bill of Rights, were proposed on September 25, 1789. They were ratified, or accepted, on December 15, 1791. They were adopted because some states refused to approve the Constitution unless a Bill of Rights, protecting individuals from various unjust acts of government was added.

Amendment 1

Freedom of religion, speech, and the press;
rights of assembly and petition

Amendment 2

Right to bear arms

Amendment 3

Housing of soldiers

Amendment 4

Search and arrest warrants

Amendment 5

Rights in criminal cases

Amendment 6

Rights to a fair trial

Amendment 7

Rights in civil cases

Amendment 8

Bails, fines, and punishments

Amendment 9

Rights retained by the people

Amendment 10

Powers retained by the states and the people

Amendment 11

Lawsuits against states

Amendment 12

Election of the President and Vice President

Amendment 13

Abolition of slavery

Amendment 14

Civil rights

Amendment 15
African-American suffrage

Amendment 16
Income taxes

Amendment 17
Direct election of senators

Amendment 18
Prohibition of liquor

Amendment 19
Women's suffrage

Amendment 20
Terms of the President and Congress

Amendment 21
Repeal of prohibition

Amendment 22
Presidential term limits

Amendment 23
Suffrage in the District of Columbia

Amendment 24

Poll taxes

Amendment 25

Presidential disability and succesion

Amendment 26

Suffrage for eighteen-year-olds

Amendment 27

Congressional salaries

Chapter Notes

Introduction

1. Alfred H. Knight, *The Life of the Law* (New York: Crown Publishers, Inc., 1996), p. 4.

2. *Application of Gault,* 387 U.S. 1, 62–63 (1967) (J. Black, concurring).

Chapter 1. What Is the Bill of Rights?

1. *Everson* v. *Board of Education,* 330 U.S. 1 (1947).

2. *Sherbert* v. *Verner,* 374 U.S. 398 (1963).

3. *Employment Division* v. *Smith,* 494 U.S. 872 (1990).

4. *Tinker* v. *Des Moines Independent Community School District,* 393 U.S. 503 (1969).

5. Letter to Colonel Edward Carrington, Jan. 16, 1787, Adrienne Koch and William Peden, eds. *The Life and Selected Writings of Thomas Jefferson* (New York: The Modern Library, 1998), p. 381.

6. *New York Times Co.* v. *Sullivan,* 376 U.S. 254 (1964).

7. *The New York Times,* March 29, 1960, in Anthony Lewis, *Make No Law: The Sullivan Case and the First Amendment* (New York: Vintage Books, 1992), pp. 2–3.

8. Lewis, p. 160.

9. *New York Times Co.* v. *Sullivan,* 376 U.S. 254, 270 (1964).

10. Ellen Alderman and Caroline Kennedy, *The Right to Privacy* (New York: Alfred A. Knopf, 1995), p. 157.

11. Leonard Levy, *Origins of the Bill of Rights* (New Haven: Yale University Press, 1999), pp. 137–138.

12. Bernard Schwartz, *The Great Rights of Mankind: A History of the American Bill of Rights* (New York: Oxford University Press, 1977), p. 87.

13. Levy, p. 133.

14. *People* v. *DeFore*, 242 N.Y. 13, 21, 150 N.E. 585, 587 (1926).

15. *New Jersey* v. *T.L.O.*, 469 U.S. 325 (1985).

16. Ibid., p. 340.

17. *Ferguson* v. *Charleston*, 99–936 (March 21, 2001).

18. Levy, p. 219–225.

19. Ibid., p. 203.

20. *Miranda* v. *Arizona*, 384 U.S. 436 (1966).

21. Alfred H. Knight, *The Life of the Law* (New York: Crown Publishers, Inc., 1996), p. 99.

22. Schwartz, p. 152.

23. *Goss* v. *Lopez*, 419 U.S. 565, 581 (1975).

24. *Moore* v. *City of East Cleveland*, 431 U.S. 494 (1977).

25. Ibid , p. 506.

26. *Nollan* v. *California Coastal Com'n*, 483 U.S. 825 (1987).

27. Ibid., p. 842.

28. *Coy* v. *Iowa*, 487 U.S. 1012, 1019 (1988).

29. *Gideon* v. *Wainwright*, 372 U.S. 335 (1963).

30. Levy, p. 235.

31. *Furman* v. *Georgia*, 408 U.S. 238 (1972).

32. *Gregg* v. *Georgia*, 428 U.S. 153 (1976).

33. Levy, p. 249.

34. Ibid., p. 241.

35. *Griswold* v. *Connecticut*, 381 U.S. 479 (1965).

Chapter 2. Ancestry of the Bill of Rights

1. Alfred H. Knight, *The Life of the Law,* (New York: Crown Publishers, Inc., 1996), p. 134.

2. Ibid., p. 17.

3. Bernard Schwartz, *The Great Rights of Mankind: A History of the American Bill of Rights* (New York: Oxford University Press, 1977), pp. 22–23.

4. Ibid., p. 33.

5. Ibid., p. 34.

6. Ibid., p. 41.

7. Howard Zinn, *A People's History of the United States,* 2nd ed. (New York: HarperPerennial, 1995), p. 60.

8. Ibid., p. 73.

9. Schwartz, p. 66.

Chapter 3. How the Constitution and the Bill of Rights Developed

1. Catherine Drinker Bowen, *The Story of the Constitutional Convention: May to September 1787* (Boston: Little, Brown and Company, 1966), p. 9.

2. Bernard Schwartz, *The Great Rights of Mankind: A History of the American Bill of Rights* (New York: Oxford University Press 1977) p. 104.

3. Alfred H. Knight, *The Life of the Law* (New York: Crown Publishers, Inc., 1996), p. 127.

4. Ibid.

5. Bowen, p. 245.

6. Knight, p. 127.

7. Jefferson to Madison Nov. 18, 1788 in James Morton Smith, ed., *The Republic of Letters: The Correspondence between Jefferson and Madison 1776–1826* (New York: W.W. Norton & Co., 1995), p. 567.

8. Peter Irons, *A People's History of the Supreme Court* (New York: Penguin Books, 1999), p. 59.

9. Ibid., p. 60.

10. Ibid.

11. Schwartz, p. 125.

12. Ibid., p. 123.

13. Ibid., p. 129.

Chapter 4. The Father of the Bill of Rights

1. Isaac Kramnick, ed., *The Federalist Papers*, Federalist 84, p. 476.

2. Ibid.

3. Ibid.

4. Article VI, Section 3 provides in part: "but no religious test shall ever be required as a Qualification to any Office or public Trust under the United States."

5. Article I, Section 9(3) provides: "No Bill of Attainder or ex post facto Law shall be passed."

6. Thomas Jefferson to James Madison, December 20, 1787, in James Morton Smith, ed., *The Republic of Letters: The Correspondence between Jefferson and Madison 1776–1826* (New York: W. W. Norton & Co., 1995), p. 513.

7. Alexis De Tocqueville, *Democracy in America*, Richard D. Hefner, ed. (New York: Penguin Books, 1956), pp. 113–129.

8. Ibid., p. 100.

9. Ibid., p. 75.

10. Helen E. Veit et al., eds. *Creating the Bill of Rights: The Documentary Record from the First Federal Congress* (Baltimore: John Hopkins University Press, 1991), p. 73.

11. Ibid., p. 78.

Chapter 5. Amending the Constitution

1. Helen E. Veit et al., eds. *Creating the Bill of Rights: The Documentary Record from the First Federal Congress* (Baltimore: John Hopkins University Press, 1991), p. 73.

2. Ibid., p. 82.

3. Ibid., p. 83.

4. Ibid.

5. Ibid., p. 84.

6. Ibid., p. 87.

7. Ibid., p. 90.

8. Ibid., p. 117.

9. Ibid., p. 118.

10. Robert A. Goldwin, *From Parchment to Power: How James Madison Used the Bill of Rights to Save the Constitution* (Washington D.C.: The AEI Press, 1997), p. 131–135.

11. Veit, p. 201.

12. Ibid., p. 36.

13. Ibid., p. 207.

14. Ibid., p. 209.

15. "James Madison to Richard Peters, August 19, 1789, in Veit et al., p. 281–282.

16. Bernard Schwartz, *The Great Rights of Mankind: A History of the American Bill of Rights* (New York: Oxford University Press, 1977), p. 187.

17. Goldwin, p. 168.

18. Ibid., p. 175.

19. Veit, p. 85.

20. Ibid., p. 188.

21. *Barron* v. *City of Baltimore*, 32 U.S. 243 (1833).

22. Ibid., p. 250.

Chapter 6. The Bill of Rights in Action

1. *Tinker* v. *Des Moines Independent Community School District*, 393 U.S. 503 (1969).

2. *Bethel School District No. 403* v. *Fraser*, 478 U.S. 675 (1986).

3. Ibid., p. 682.

4. *Hazelwood School District* v. *Kuhlmeier*, 484 U.S. 260 (1988).

5. *Texas* v. *Johnson*, 491 U.S. 397 (1989).

6. Ibid.

7. Ibid., p. 418.

8. Ibid., p. 414.

9. *United States* v. *Eichman*, 496 U.S. 310 (1990).

10. Ibid., p. 318.

11. *Engel* v. *Vitale*, 370 U.S. 421 (1962).

12. The U.S. Supreme Court is composed of nine justices. However, Justices Felix Frankfurter and Byron White took no part in the decision of this case. Therefore, there were only seven Justices.

13. *Engel* v. *Vitale*, 370 U.S. 421, 425 (1962).

14. Ibid., p. 449.

15. 530 U.S. 290 (2000).

16. Ibid., p. 304.

17. Ibid., p. 2283 (J. Rehnquist dissenting).

18. Ibid., p. 963.

19. 389 U.S. 347 (1967).

20. Ibid., p. 359.

21. Ibid., p. 360.

22. Ibid., p. 1379.

23. Ibid., p. 455.

24. Ibid., p. 479.

25. *Dickerson* v. *U.S.*, 530 U.S. 428 (2000).

26. *Doggett* v. *United States*, 505 U.S. 647 (1992).

27. *California* v. *Green*, 399 U.S. 149, 158 (1970).

28. Anthony Lewis, *Make No Law: The Sullivan Case and the First Amendment* (New York: Vintage Books, 1992), p. 10.

29. Ibid., p. 344.

30. *Stack* v. *Boyle*, 342 U.S. 1, 4 (1951).

31. Ibid., p. 6.

32. *U.S.* v. *Bajakajian*, 524 U.S. 321, 337-338 (1998).

33. Ibid., p. 339.

34. *McClesky* v. *Kemp*, 481 U.S. 279 (1986).

35. Ibid., p. 312.

36. *Callins* v. *Collins*, 510 U.S. 1141, 1145 (1994) (Blackmun, J., dissenting).

37. Ibid., p. 1130.

38. Ibid.

39. *Ingrahamm* v. *Wright*, 430 U.S. 651, 663 (1977)

40. *Griswold* v. *Connecticut*, 381 U.S. 479 (1965).

41. Ibid., p. 499.

42. *Roe* v. *Wade*, 410 U.S. 113 (1973).

43. Ibid., p. 933.

Chapter 7. Conclusion

1. Helen E. Veit et al., eds. *Creating the Bill of Rights: The Documentary Record from the First Federal Congress* (Baltimore: John Hopkins University Press, 1991), p. 78.

2. Geoffrey R. Stone et al. *Constitutional Law* 2nd ed. (Boston: Little Brown & Company, 1991), p. 784.

3. *West Virginia* v. *Barnette*, 319 U.S. 624, 637 (1943).

4. *U.S.* v. *Rabinowitz*, 339 U.S. 56, 69 (1951) (J. Frankfurter, dissenting).

5. Nat Hentoff, *Living the Bill of Rights: How to be an Authentic American* (Sacramento: University of California Press, 1999), p. 197.

6. *Olmstead* v. *U.S.*, 277 U.S. 438, 479 (1928).

7. David L. Hudson, Jr., *Censorship of Student Internet Speech: The Effect of Diminishing Student Rights, Fear of the Internet and Columbine*, 2000 L. REV. M.S.U.–D.C.L. 199, 221–222.

Further Reading

Collier, Christopher, and James Lincoln Collier. *Decision in Philadelphia: The Constitutional Convention of 1787.* New York: Ballantine Books, 1986.

The Commission on the Bicentennial of the United States Constitution. *1791–1991: The Bill of Rights and Beyond.* Washington, D.C.: U.S. Congress, 1991.

Dudley, William, ed. *The Creation of the Constitution: Opposing Viewpoints.* San Diego, Calif.: Greenhaven Press, Inc., 1995.

Ellis, Joseph J. *Founding Brothers: The Revolutionary Generation.* New York, Vintage Books, 2000.

Faber, Doris and Harold Faber. *We the People: The Story of the United States Constitution Since 1787.* New York: Charles Scribner's Sons, 1987.

West, Thomas G. *Vindicating the Founders: Race, Sex, Class and Justice in the Origins of America.* Lanham, Maryland: Rowman and Littlefield Publishers, 2001.

Internet Addresses

ConstitutionFacts.com.
<http://www.constitutionfacts.com>

National Archives and Records Administration. *The Bill of Rights.*
<http://www.archives.gov/exhibit_hall/charters_of_freedom/bill_of_rights/bill_of_rights.html>

National Constitution Center
<http://www.constitutioncenter.org/sections/kids/kids_main.asp>

Index